# CULTURES OF THE WORLD
# Afghanistan

Cavendish
Square
New York

Published in 2014 by Cavendish Square Publishing, LLC
303 Park Avenue South, Suite 1247, New York, NY 10010

Third Edition

This publication is published with arrangement with Marshall Cavendish International (Asia) Pte Ltd.

Website: cavendishsq.com

Cultures of the World is a registered trademark of Times Publishing Limited.

This publication represents the opinions and views of the author based on his or her personal experience, knowledge, and research. The information in this book serves as a general guide only. The author and publisher have used their best efforts in preparing this book and disclaim liability rising directly or indirectly from the use and application of this book.

CPSIA Compliance Information: Batch #WS13CSQ

All websites were available and accurate when this book was sent to press.

**Library of Congress Cataloging-in-Publication Data**
Ali, Sharifah Enayat, 1943–
  Afghanistan / Sharifah Enayat Ali and Josie Elias. — 3rd ed.
      p. cm. — (Cultures of the world)
  Includes bibliographical references and index.
  Audience: Grades 4–6.
  Summary: "Provides comprehensive information on the geography, history,
wildlife, governmental structure, economy, cultural diversity, peoples,
religion, and culture of Afghanistan"—Provided by publisher.
  ISBN 978-1-60870-866-6 (hardcover) ISBN 978-1-62712-157-6 (paperback) ISBN 978-1-60870-872-7 (ebook)
  1. Afghanistan--Juvenile literature. I. Elias, Josie. II. Title.

DS351.5.A44 2013

Writers: Sharifah Enayat Ali and Josie Elias
Editors: Deborah Grahame-Smith, Mindy Pang
Copyreader: Tara Tomczyk
Designers: Nancy Sabato, Lynn Chin
Cover picture researcher: Tracey Engel
Picture researcher: Joshua Ang

**PICTURE CREDITS**
Cover: © Alison Wright / Corbis
alt.TYPE / REUTERS: 120, 121 • Audrius Tomonis - www.banknotes.com: 135 • Corbis / Click Photos: 115 • Getty Images: 38, 39, 81, 118 • Inmagine.com: 1, 3, 5, 7, 9, 10, 12, 13, 14, 17, 19, 24, 26, 27, 28, 29, 32, 33, 34, 36, 42, 45, 48, 52, 54, 56, 60, 62, 63, 65, 68, 73, 74, 78, 83, 84, 85, 87, 88, 90, 92, 96, 98, 99, 102, 104, 105, 108, 110, 111, 113, 114, 116, 124, 126, 129, 131 • Jane Sweeney / Lonely Planet Images: 18 • Marshall Cavendish Archives (Yeo Chong Jin): 130 • S.K. Vemmer (U.S. Department of State) / Wikimedia Commons: 22 • Stephane Victor / Lonely Planet Images: 31 • Tony Wheeler / Lonely Planet Images: 11

**PRECEDING PAGE**
A view of the Herat River in west Afghanistan.

Printed in the United States of America

# CONTENTS

# AFGHANISTAN TODAY

**A**FGHANISTAN, OR "LAND OF THE AFGHANS," A PATCHWORK OF diverse kingdoms, came into existence as a single entity only in the 18th century. Lying at the crossroads between Europe and the Far East, a steady stream of conquerors, adventurers, and soldiers of fortune has arrived there through the narrow passes of the Hindu Kush throughout the centuries.

The Afghans had often been called "giant killers." Both Darius I of Persia and Alexander the Great of Macedonia found them to be a formidable foe, as did, much later, the British and the Russians. However, the last two decades of the 20th century, from the Soviet occupation to the overthrow of the severe Taliban regime in 2001, left Afghanistan devastated—its farmlands were ravaged, pastures and roads were riddled with land mines, and cities were ruined.

In December 2001 Hamid Karzai, an ethnic Pashtun and leader of one of the largest tribes in southern Afghanistan, was sworn in as chairman of a six-month interim government. In June 2002 Hamid Karzai was elected as president of the new interim government by the *Loya Jirga* (law-yah jorhr-GAH) or Grand Assembly. By 2004 rival Afghan factions agreed on a constitution, which finally paved the way for democratic elections. Shortly afterward 23 donor nations pledged a total of $8.2 billion in aid to Afghanistan over three years. However, there is a wide gap between the pledges made and the actual assistance delivered. Between 2002 and 2005 only $3.3 billion was spent, and fewer than $1 billion worth of projects were actually completed. This is the Afghanistan of today, more than 10 years since the end of the civil war and the fall of the Taliban, the majority of the population is still working hard at rebuilding the basic infrastructure of the country, improving health and education, renovating factories, building reliable transport networks, and trying to get the country to the stage where it can be in control of its own security operations and not dependent on foreign aid. Despite new leadership and efforts to rebuild, Afghans still do not live in peace.

A lack of security is one of the country's biggest problems. Businessmen and women have been randomly kidnapped and held for ransom by gangs. The level of violence has increased and opium cultivation is still a primary source of income for many Afghan farmers, particularly in the southern parts of Afghanistan where the Taliban still have influence. The number of drug addicts has increased to around 1 million, out of a population of approximately 31 million. Opium production, which increased for many years following the fall of the Taliban, has begun to show a decline as more farmers are encouraged to grow crops such as wheat, fruit, and vegetables. Most of the opium is grown in areas where security is worst.

Foreign troops are stationed in Afghanistan with the intention of helping it to overcome its problem with national security. The tactics of the Taliban have changed. They now disrupt national security by planting improvised explosive devices (IEDs) and carrying out suicide attacks, often injuring or killing Afghan civilians. The United States and the international community are spending billions of dollars and sending relief workers into this war-torn country to help with projects as diverse as reopening power plants to planting trees, clearing land mines, and digging wells. Progress has also been made in training and educating Afghan police and military personnel. The number of officers and noncommissioned officers in the police force increased from 42,500 in 2009 to 61,850 in 2011. The same applies to the army. Between 2009 and 2011 the number of officers and noncommissioned officers grew from 40,900 to 66,800. Training and education are essential in developing leaders but experience is also essential and that requires time. Afghans need

to be able to be in control of the security of their own country in order for the foreign troop withdrawal to take place successfully without the country reverting to civil war and unrest.

However, the presence of foreign troops in Afghanistan has also been controversial. In February 2012 a number of copies of the Koran were burned in an incinerator pit at Bagram airbase by coalition forces. This resulted in a series of attacks, including a suicide car bomb attack at Jalalabad airport that killed six civilians, an Afghan soldier, and two local guards. Taliban insurgents claimed responsibility for the blast, saying it was in revenge for the burning of the Korans. U.S. soldiers were also wounded in a grenade attack during an anti-U.S. demonstration at their base in northern Kunduz province. In March 2012 a U.S. military soldier, Army Staff Sergeant Robert Bales, was charged with killing 17 Afghan civilians, 9 of whom were children. The massacre took place in the Panjwai district of Kandahar province where the U.S. soldier was based. These incidents have upset relations between Afghanistan and the United States at a time when American commanders are trying to help stabilize the country in preparation for an eventual U.S. withdrawal of troops from the country.

Afghanistan remains one of the world's poorest nations but many Afghanis believe that they are better off now than they were in 2001. International aid has donated funds for local projects to improve roads, water supply, health and education but infrastructure is still a major concern. A third of the country has no access to regular electricity supplies. Traffic in the

Built by King Amanullah Khan to modernize Afghanistan, the European-style Darul Aman Palace, or "abode of peace," located just outside Kabul, was ruined during the civil war.

cities is a huge problem, causing not just congestion on the roads but also air pollution. Kabul police estimate that there are 500,000 vehicles on the roads of Kabul alone, whereas 10 years ago there were roughly 50,000. In rural areas hundreds of miles of roads have been built, though not necessarily paved. There is still extensive use of donkeys and horse carts for transportation purposes, but cars are slowly becoming more widespread even in the villages.

The infant mortality and maternal mortality rates are still high, but international foreign aid has contributed to the building of new hospitals and health-care centers. Child immunization programs are saving an estimated 35,000 lives a year as children are immunized against diseases, such as measles and polio.

The adult literacy rate in Afghanistan is one of the worst in the world but the youth literacy rate is slowly showing signs of improvement, as new schools have been built, damaged schools have been reopened, more teachers have been trained, and children are once again encouraged (and able) to go to school. The Ministry of Education has estimated that today 8.5 million students go to school. Under the Taliban, women were not allowed to vote and girls were not permitted to go to school. Rates of literacy for both boys and girls are now rising, and women are allowed to work. Today women represent almost 28 percent of Afghanistan's National Parliament, an astonishing 9 percent higher than the world average of women in parliament.

In 2008 the UN announced that 68 percent of the Afghanistan population was under the age of 25. In Kabul city Internet cafés are packed with this new generation born in the 1990s. These people never knew the civil war and they barely remember the Taliban regime. They are an educated force skilled in new technologies; they use Facebook and Twitter while their parents may have been illiterate farmers. Some children, even daughters, have been sent abroad for higher education through various scholarship funding programs. Previously, in such a tribal and traditional society, this would have been impossible.

According to the Ministry of Information and Communication there are approximately 17 million mobile phone users in Afghanistan and five wireless companies cover approximately 80 percent of the country. There are hundreds of FM radio stations today whereas a few years ago there were only three. These stations broadcast 24 hours a day. There are more than 50 private television stations and more than 50 newspapers. These improvements in communication have resulted in some changes in society. The tribal elders, although still widely respected, are losing control over society as the youth becomes more educated. The Afghan youth have, in some respects, progressed beyond their elders and clerics through their wider experiences, learning, and knowledge. This new, younger generation wants democracy to continue, and they want human rights and the rule of law to replace old tribal codes and lifestyles. In the Beijing Olympic Games in 2008, Rohullah Nikpai won a bronze medal in the taekwondo event. This was Afghanistan's first ever Olympic medal win and it thrilled the entire country, especially the youngsters who saw that it was worthwhile to aim for the best and to aspire to a bright future.

Afghanistan's social and economic development has been slow but steady. Infrastructure and reconstruction projects, mainly financed by the international community, have lifted hundreds of thousands of Afghans from absolute poverty and provided them with the opportunity to earn wages. Initiatives introduced range from poultry farming and fruit farming to higher education and vocational training.

A study center in Afghanistan provides Internet facilities for youths.

Many people in Afghanistan are worried about the future. Dependent now on foreign aid and establishing the foundations for reconstruction, Afghanistan is at a turning point in its history. There are concerns not only about political stability of Afghanistan as the United States and international forces are due to pull out in 2014, but there are also major concerns about the economy, which is heavily dependent on foreign aid. Of the total government expenditure of $17 billion in 2010, only $1.9 billion came from Afghanistan's own sources of revenue. The present economy depends almost entirely on the development funds provided by the United States, Europe, Japan, Australia, Canada, and other nations. The money spent supporting the security environment is immense. After 2014 most of this money will fade away. It is unknown how much the donor nations will continue to contribute after 2014. Most nations are turned off by the immense corruption of the Karzai regime. By then it is hoped that the country will be able to manage its own national security and remain on the path to a bright, safe, and secure future for all its citizens. There is hope for the peace that has always eluded conflict-ridden Afghanistan and its people.

# GEOGRAPHY

The gorgeous Band-E-Amir, or "Dam of the King," crater lake in the Bamian province of Afghanistan.

HE COUNTRY OF AFGHANISTAN lies between latitudes 29° and 38°N and longitudes 61° and 75°E in southwestern Asia. With a land area of about 251,827 square miles (652,230 square kilometers), it is approximately the size of Texas. Much of the country is covered by the mountain ranges of the Hindu Kush, which rise to heights of 24,000 feet (7,315 meters) in the east. In addition there are extensive deserts and plains.

Shahr-e-Gholghola in the ancient city of Bamiyan. Vast stretches of perilous mountains, arid valleys, and dry desert land add to the hot and harsh climate of Afghanistan.

The Panjshir
Valley, or "Valley
of the Five Lions,"
is divided by the
Panjshir River.
The valley is
home to many
of the ethnic
Tajik communities
in Afghanistan.

Afghanistan is a landlocked country. To the north lie the Central Asian republics that once belonged to the former Soviet Union—Uzbekistan, Tajikistan, and Turkmenistan. Part of the boundary with these republics, about 680 miles (1,094 km) long, is formed by the Oxus River, now called the Amu Dar'ya. To the east and southeast, separated by the Durand Line, lies Pakistan. To the west lies Iran, while the Chinese province of Sinkiang, also known as Xinjiang, borders the Wakhan Mountains in the northeast.

## TOPOGRAPHY

Afghanistan can be divided broadly into three regions—the northern plains, the central mountains, and the southern plateau.

**NORTHERN PLAINS** This region has some of the most fertile land in Afghanistan and is the country's major agricultural area. Because rainfall is inadequate, however, only river valleys and regions where water is available can be cultivated.

The name *Amu
Dar'ya (Amudariya)*
means "Mother
of Rivers."

Irrigation systems have been built along some rivers. The Kokcha and the Kunduz—two important tributaries of the Amu Dar'ya River flowing from the Hindu Kush—enable farmers to cultivate rice and cotton. Semi-nomads also raise sheep and goats on the vast grasslands here.

**CENTRAL MOUNTAINS** Afghanistan's mountain ranges are an extension of the Himalayan Mountains and cover about two-thirds of the country. The Hindu Kush, which extends across the country from the southeast to the northeast, forms the backbone of Afghanistan's central mountains.

The famed snowcapped Kohi Baba Mountains, which rise to almost 17,000 feet (5,182 m), make up the southwestern branch of the Hindu Kush. The highest mountain here is the Shah Fuladi (16,873 feet, or 5,143 m). The tallest peaks in the country, however, are found near the northeastern border with Pakistan, where the Nowshak (24,557 feet, or 7,485 m), Afghanistan's highest mountain, is located. The northeastern part of the highlands, including the Wakhan, is geologically active. In the 20th century alone more than a dozen significantly damaging earthquakes occurred in the area around Kabul.

The 435-mile (700-km) Kabul River is a vital source of water here, as its tributaries irrigate some of the most productive agricultural land in the country. To the east the Khyber Pass enables travelers to traverse the daunting terrain of the Hindu Kush into Pakistan. Another mountain route, the Baroghil Pass, links the Wakhan Valley with northern Pakistan.

The Kohi Baba range of the Hindu Kush mountains rises between and Mazar-i-Sharif in Afghanistan.

**SOUTHERN PLATEAU** The southwestern region consists primarily of desert and semi-desert land. The largest deserts here are the Registan, Dashti Margo, and Dashti Khash. These barren areas, which cover over 50,000 square miles (130,000 square km), lie between 1,500 and 3,000 feet (450 and 900 m) above sea level. The entire region is bisected by the 715-mile (1,150-km) Helmand River, which flows from the Hindu Kush to Lake Helmand, a vast, marshy lake in the Sistan Basin on the Iranian border. Lake Helmand, one of the few lakes in

A desert in Afghanistan. The climate in these inhospitable barren lands tends to fluctuate greatly. This is why camels are bred for transportation, especially by the nomadic peoples.

Afghanistan, expands and contracts with the seasonal flow of its rivers. In the extreme southwest of the great plateau is the marshland of Gawd-i-Zirreh.

## CLIMATE

Severe winters and long, hot summers characterize Afghanistan's climate. The weather is influenced more by its high altitude than by its latitude. From December to March air masses come from the cold north, bringing very cold weather and snow to the mountains.

The climate during the months from June to September is very hot and dry, although eastern Afghanistan receives some rain. Nights can be very cold, however, even in summer. Little rain falls at lower altitudes, and the plains are extremely dry. Precipitation in the country averages just 9.84 inches (25 centimeters) a year. The southwest is even more arid than the east. Strong winds, such as the "wind of 120 days," blow during the summer months along the Iran-Afghanistan border, and commonly cause sandstorms. In the southwestern deserts the temperature difference between day and night can be very extreme. In the summer, for example, water freezes at night, despite noon temperatures of up to 120°F (49°C).

Only in areas like Kabul, which are situated at higher altitudes and are sheltered, the climate is relatively pleasant. Kabul's yearly temperature ranges between -4°F and 86°F (-20°C and 30°C).

# FLORA AND FAUNA

Less than 1.5 percent of Afghanistan is forested. The forests thrive mainly in the inaccessible Nuristan Province of eastern Afghanistan and include pine, cypress, and oak. The most prized tree is the deodar cedar (*Cedrus deodara*) that Afghans use to build furniture and houses. Stunted pines and oaks are also much sought after by woodcutters. Forests that have been cut do not regenerate. They revert to shrubland mainly because of the pressure of livestock grazing and higher soil temperature. In spring flowers such as the cowslip and anemone bloom in the valleys and hillsides. As summer approaches, tulips appear, followed by petunias, sunflowers, marigolds, honeysuckles, dahlias, and geraniums. The semi-desert areas are characterized by lush, shallow-rooted herbaceous vegetation early in the year, which soon dries up and dies. The desert basin plants are mostly halophytic (salt-loving) and xerophytic (dry-loving) shrubs and herbs.

Animals and birds, in the Hindu Kush, typical of the nearby Himalayas include the Himalayan snowcock (*Tetraogallus himalayensis*), Himalayan ibex (*Capra sibirica hemalayanus*), Himalayan brown bear (*Ursos arctos*), snow leopard (*Uncia uncia*), and the piping hare (*Lagomys roylei*). The Argali or Marco Polo sheep (*Ovis ammon poli*) inhabit the mountain areas of Central Asia above 3,280 feet (1,000 meters). The Argali is a vulnerable species threatened by habitat loss from the grazing of domestic sheep and hunted for their highly prized horns.

In the northern plains can be found the fauna of the steppes (level, treeless land), such as bustards and the suslik, a ground squirrel. In the western deserts thrive the creatures characteristic of the Caspian Sea—gazelles, coursers (a long-legged bird), flamingos, and swallow plovers. Camels are native to the region: the single-humped Arvana dromedary is common on the plains, and the double-humped Bactrian camel is found in the mountains. Wild pigs, which the Afghans call *khooki washi*, are found in tamarisk groves.

The cheetah, leopard, mongoose, and other animals of the Indian subcontinent are found in southern and eastern Afghanistan. The macaque, a type of monkey, is found in the forested areas of Nuristan, near the Pakistani border. Leopards, otters, and foxes are sometimes hunted for their pelts, which are sold to make blankets and coats.

The Helmand River is the longest river flowing almost entirely within Afghanistan. It is about 715 miles (1,150 km) long and, together with its tributaries, drains the whole of southern Afghanistan. The Amu Dar'ya, which forms part of the boundary between Afghanistan and the Central Asian republics, is the major river in the north. Rising in the Hindu Kush, it flows for about 1,578 miles (2,540 km) to empty into the Aral Sea in Turkmenistan.

Fish abound in the rivers. To the north of the Hindu Kush, a native brown trout (*Salmo trutta*), locally known as *kalmahi*, can be found. Fifty-four percent of the fish species found in Afghanistan are minnows and carp, and 25 percent are loaches. Only one species of fish, the *Tryplophysa farwelli*, is known to be endemic to Afghanistan.

However, the country's once abundant biodiversity is diminishing greatly due to the damaging effects of war and environmental degradation. Flamingos have not bred successfully for a number of years and the last Siberian crane was seen in 1986. Hunting for sport, for meat, or simply to supply the illegal fur trade in Kabul has placed the natural wildlife heritage of Afghanistan under threat.

## CITIES

**KABUL** Kabul is strategically located close to the Khyber Pass. Nestled 5,905 feet (1,800 m) above sea level on a well-sheltered plateau, Kabul is one of the highest capital cities in the world.

Bare, rocky mountains rise in the south and west. Because of the altitude, Kabul's climate is not unlike that of Denver, Colorado—invigorating, with bright sunshine and thin, clear air. The summers are dry, but there is rain in spring and heavy snowfall in winter, when the cultural and economic center of the country is often snowbound.

This city was once full of bazaars and narrow alleys with shops selling a wide variety of merchandise, from exotic carpets to nuts, fruits, grains, and an assortment of handcrafted items and garments. The modern parts of the city had wide boulevards, carrying an incredible mixture of traffic—trucks, buses, jeeps, and automobiles moving alongside camels, donkeys, and horse carts laden high with a vast array of goods and passengers.

Two decades of continual war and political chaos left a trail of devastation in Kabul. Most of the city's infrastructure services, such as electricity, water, and sanitation, were destroyed. Moreover little had been done to build new roads and to improve telecommunications in the country. Kabul's trolleybus service came to a halt in December 1992 when a civil war started. A plan to reinstall the trolleybuses that the city once had is under evaluation. Kabul has a public transportation system of public buses, called Millie Bus, which takes commuters on daily routes to destinations throughout the city. Distinctive

yellow taxis are available for private hire by individuals or groups. An express bus runs from the city center to Kabul International Airport. There is a bus service between Pakistan and Afghanistan, but the timetable is erratic.

Kabul's estimated population of 800,000 before the war swelled to more than 3.3 million in 2012 after the return of millions of refugees. Population pressure in the city has been exacerbated by the exodus of the rural population to the cities. With many homes and buildings destroyed during the recent decades of violence, there is a very severe lack of shelter. Efforts made to improve the living conditions of its residents have been insufficient, and many still do not have access to safe drinking water, sanitation, electricity, and other basic amenities. Pollution levels are also appalling.

Informal settlements shelter approximately 80 percent of Kabul's population and cover 69 percent of the city's residential land. Housing projects and policies have been undertaken by the new independent government, with the aid of international humanitarian organizations, such as the United Nations High Commission for Refugees (UNHCR). Aid efforts have been made to improve the poor standard of living of the people.

Among the most noticeable developments has been the resuscitation of the bazaars and street life in Kabul. Whereas the primary color in Kabul's streets was dusty gray during the period of the Taliban, colors have returned to store fronts and to the apparel of those who frequent them. The return of music and the enthusiastic bargaining of Kabulis have restored to life once-dormant shops and neighborhoods.

An aerial view of Kabul. For centuries, Kabul has stood in the path of great invaders, from Alexander the Great and Genghis Khan to Tamerlane and Nadir Shah.

The Gaur Shad's Mausoleum at Mousallah Complex is one of Herat's main architectural icons.

**KANDAHAR** Kandahar is the capital of Kandahar Province, one of the richest provinces in Afghanistan. It lies on a plain next to the Tarnak River at an elevation of about 3,300 feet (1,100 m). The area around Kandahar is irrigated farmland where fruits, such as grapes, melons, and pomegranates, are grown. Food processing is an important industry in the city, which also has many textile factories to process the large quantities of wool produced in the area around the city.

Kandahar was the first capital of modern Afghanistan, and it is the country's second-largest city. It has wide, cobbled main streets. Unlike Kabul, its bazaars are roomy and open. The houses have arched doorways and are made of baked bricks laid over wooden scaffolding, which is used over and over again as wood is scarce.

The city is free of winter snow and lies on the shortest air route between Europe and Asia. It has an international airport that has largely become a military facility. An excellent road, which is open in all weather, connects the city to Pakistan.

**MAZAR-I-SHARIF** Mazar-i-Sharif is the largest city in northern Afghanistan and is situated 35 miles (56 km) south of the border with Uzbekistan at an elevation of 1,250 feet (380 m). It is an important and strategic trading center for the north and lies just 13 miles (21 km) southwest of the Amu Dar'ya River. It is best known throughout the Islamic world as one of the reputed sites of the Tomb of Hazrat Ali, the son-in-law of Prophet Muhammad.

Mazar-i-Sharif is irrigated by the Balkh River and is one of the most fertile regions in Afghanistan. Cotton, grain, and fruit are grown in the area and silk and cotton textiles are manufactured in the city. It is connected by air and road to Kabul, which lies 200 miles (320 km) to the southeast and is the country's main transit point for Central Asian trade.

**GHAZNI** Ghazni, which lies 80 miles (129 km) south of Kabul, was the resplendent capital of Sultan Mahmud, a ruler of the Ghazni dynasty, in the 11th century. Today it is an important commercial and industrial center dealing in furs, livestock, and silk. Afghan sheepskin coats are made in the city.

**HERAT**  Herat is situated in the Harirud Valley, a major fruit- and grain-producing area in western Afghanistan. Its proximity to Iran made it the center for Persian art and architecture during the 15th and 16th centuries. The old city is surrounded by a large moat, massive walls, and many towers. Today a modern area has grown around the walls. Herat is famous for its carpets and woolen cloth.

## INTERNET LINKS

**www.summitpost.org/the-hindukush/180975**

This site contains information, facts, and figures on the Hindu Kush mountain range, especially on climbing, hiking, and mountaineering.

**http://pubs.usgs.gov/fs/2007/3027/pdf/FS07-3027_508.pdf**

This U.S. Geological Survey website has detailed information on earthquakes in Afghanistan, including a preliminary assessment of seismic hazard, which incorporates data from thousands of earthquakes.

**http://riveroxus.blogspot.com/**

This is the expedition report for the Royal Geographical Society in London. It tells the story of a journey undertaken in 2007 to find the source of the River Oxus in the Wakhan Corridor of northeastern Afghanistan.

**www.cfr.org/pakistan/troubled-afghan-pakistani-border/p14905**

This website provides information on the troubled Afghan-Pakistani border and the creation of the Durand Line—how Kabul has never recognized the line as an international border.

In the mid-1980s Herat lost almost two-thirds of its population as residents fled the war-torn city. Today Herat, located near Iran, has attracted a large number of migrants from drought-affected areas and an influx of returned refugees. There is a wide disparity between the standards of living of its permanent residents and the refugees.

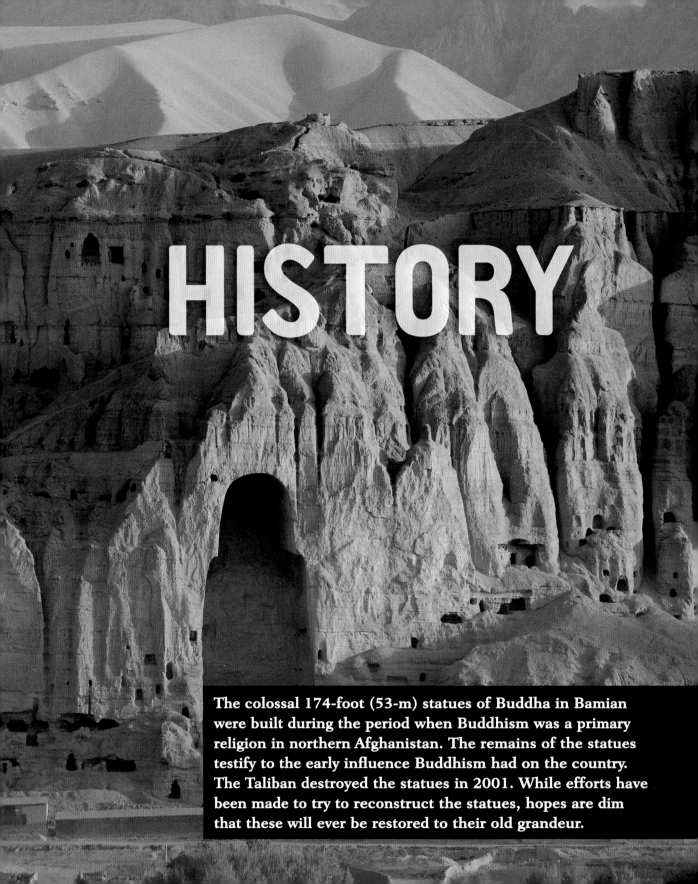

# HISTORY

The colossal 174-foot (53-m) statues of Buddha in Bamian were built during the period when Buddhism was a primary religion in northern Afghanistan. The remains of the statues testify to the early influence Buddhism had on the country. The Taliban destroyed the statues in 2001. While efforts have been made to try to reconstruct the statues, hopes are dim that these will ever be restored to their old grandeur.

**2**

AFGHANISTAN AS WE KNOW IT today emerged as a nation in 1747, when it was unified under the leadership of Ahmed Shah. This rugged land, which lies at the crossroads between Europe and China, has a long and turbulent history of invasion and warfare.

## EARLY CIVILIZATION

Archaeological finds since 1949 reveal that humans had settled in northern Afghanistan some 50,000 years ago. Historians also believe that Afghanistan may have been one of the areas where humans first domesticated animals and raised such plants as wheat and barley.

Agricultural villages that provided food to Mohenjo-Daro, Harappa, and the other great regional centers of the Indus River Valley civilizations may have been in Afghanistan.

## ACHAEMENID EMPIRE

The ancient land of Bactria in northern Afghanistan first appeared in recorded history in about 550 B.C., when the Persian monarch Cyrus the Great incorporated it into his Achaemenid Empire.

Darius the Great, who ruled from 522 to 486 B.C., and his son Xerxes, who ruled from 486 to 465 B.C., expanded the empire farther to include provinces in and around Afghanistan, creating the largest empire of the ancient world.

The American archaeologist Louis Dupree discovered tools and flints from the Mousterian period (Middle Paleolithic) in a site called the Cave of the Dead Sheep in the foothills near Gurziwan. These finds and others have established that the ancient history of Afghanistan is at least 50,000 years old.

## GREEK RULE

Alexander the Great defeated the Persians in 328 B.C., when he led his army north through the Hindu Kush passes and spent a year conquering the lands on both sides of the Amu Dar'ya River. Following Alexander's conquests, the Greek empire ruled the region until Alexander's death in 323 B.C. The subsequent regency period of Philip III Arrhidaeus (Alexander's feeble-minded half-brother), and then the infant Alexander IV of Macedonia, ended in 310 B.C.

**The Qala Iktyaruddin citadel in Herat was originally built by Alexander the Great in 330 B.C.**

Following the regency period and several wars, Bactria became part of the Seleucid Empire. Much of the land south of the Hindu Kush fell under the control of Chandragupta, who had established the Mauryan Empire in northern India. Chandragupta was later succeeded by his grandson Ashoka, who established several important Buddhist religious centers in the Hindu Kush.

In 185 B.C. the large Mauryan Empire disintegrated. The Greeks in the north, who had by then established an independent Greco-Bactrian kingdom, quickly took advantage of its decline and moved south across the Hindu Kush.

When the Bactrian Empire subsequently broke up, Greek rule in Afghanistan ended. However, their influence on art and culture remained. The combination of Grecian, Mauryan, and Kushan cultures produced what is today known as Gandharan art, found in the cities and monasteries of the Kabul Valley. Gandharan art is a style of Buddhist visual art.

## SUCCESSION OF CONQUERORS

As a young man, from age 13 to 16, Alexander the Great was taught by the Athenian philosopher Aristotle of Stagira.

The Saka, nomadic invaders from Central Asia, pushed the Greeks out of Bactria and northwest India, occupied Sakastan, and, for a brief period, ruled the land between the Helmand River and the Persian Gulf. Then the Parthians, who controlled Iran, conquered Sakastan and made it a Parthian satrapy, or province. At its peak the Parthian-ruled empire extended from Armenia to India.

The Parthians were later overthrown by the Kushans from across the Amu Dar'ya. By the middle of the first century A.D. the Kushans had crossed the Hindu Kush and were ruling the entire Kabul Valley, which was known as Gandhara. The Kushans controlled all the land from the lower Indus Valley to the Iranian border and from the Chinese Sinkiang Province to the Caspian and Aral seas.

Kanishka was the greatest of the Kushan emperors. During his reign Buddhism enjoyed its greatest influence and spread to the Far East and parts of Southeast Asia. Sculpture and art also flourished and made a great impact on the cultures of Afghanistan, India, Iran, and even China. When the Kushan dynasty ended in A.D. 220, the country became fragmented.

In the third century Ardashir founded the mighty Sassanian dynasty. The dynasty ruled over the Persian Empire for four centuries and dominated Afghanistan and Pakistan west of the Indus.

## ARRIVAL OF ISLAM

The Islamic conquest of Afghanistan has become the very essence of Afghan experience and being. The Arabs defeated the Sassanids in Persia in about A.D. 642, bringing Iran under Arab control. They crossed the Amu Dar'ya in A.D. 667 and invaded Herat. By A.D. 714 Arab control of the region up to the Indus River was complete, although pockets of tribal resistance continued for centuries.

During the caliphate of Harun al-Rashid of the Abbasid dynasty (786—809), Balkh became a great seat of learning. In the ninth century the Abbasids were displaced by three local kingdoms in quick succession—the Tahirids, Saffarids, and Samanids. The Saffarids were the first to unite the regions north and south of the Hindu Kush under one rule. They were instrumental in converting the remote groups to Islam and in promoting the use of Farsi (the language of Persia) among the people. The Samanids soon overthrew the Saffarids, and a great empire that stretched from India to Baghdad was established by A.D. 920. By A.D. 943, however, this empire had begun to disintegrate. The kings had trained Turkish slaves for military and civil use. Eventually these slaves gained influence and power over their masters.

The most important archaeological find in Afghanistan was made in 1963 when the French located the Greek city of Ai Khanoum (Alexandria on Oxus), at the confluence of the Kokcha and Darya-i-Panj rivers. This is the easternmost Greek city ever discovered and consists of several complexes. The upper town has a huge citadel, and the lower town has residential and administrative buildings, including a palace, a university, a gymnasium, and a temple.

## GHAZNAVID DYNASTY

In A.D. 962 one of the king's Turkish slaves, Alptigin, overthrew his master and became the ruler of Ghazni. Thus the Ghaznavid dynasty, which brought an era of magnificence to this region, was founded. The third ruler of this dynasty, Sultan Mahmud of Ghazni, contributed tremendously to the expansion of Islam in the region and India. Besides being a great general, successfully consolidating and expanding the dynasty's territories, he was a patron of the arts and filled his capital, Ghazni, and other cities with the best intellectuals, artists, and scientists of his time. Among the intellectuals in Mahmud's court were the poet Firdawsi, scientist-historian al-Biruni, and the historian al-Utbi. Mahmud used Afghan mercenaries in his conquest of India, where they succeeded to the throne of Delhi and the command of three important principalities. They remained renowned in India for the next 300 years for their military prowess.

After Sultan Mahmud's death in A.D. 1030, the empire declined and the dynasty was finally overthrown by the Ghorids from northwestern Afghanistan, who captured and burned the splendid city of Ghazni. The Ghorids went on to conquer India and almost forgot their homeland.

The Ghazni Victory Tower was built by Mahmud of Ghazni to commemorate his military victories.

## MONGOL RULE

In the 13th century Genghis Khan swept out of Central Asia with his Mongolian forces and mercilessly destroyed everything in his path. Wherever he passed, his armies left behind a trail of ruin and desolation.

In A.D. 1220 Genghis Khan reached the Amu Dar'ya River and invaded Balkh (only a small town today). His armies rode through the city and left it completely devastated. Nevertheless the city recovered some of its glory because it lay on one of the important trade routes in medieval times. In 1221 Herat was captured by the Mongols and Tuli, the son of Genghis Khan, ruled over it for some time, but the citizens revolted and killed the Mongol garrison chief. Extremely angered, Genghis Khan rode upon the city with 80,000

*Archaeological evidence confirming the truth of historical references to the lands of the Hindu Kush has grown steadily since World War II. Ashoka's rocks and pillars of edicts, for example, were found in 1958 and 1963 respectively, near Kandahar. Others were found in India and Pakistan.*

*Ashoka became king in about 270 B.C. The many rocks and pillars of edicts were Ashoka's way of promoting the Buddhist way of nonviolent life, and through them he imparted moral values and the virtue of religious tolerance to his subjects. They were very much like billboards in the United States today, except that he was advertising a way of life instead of a product.*

*The edicts in Afghanistan were written in Greek and Aramaic. Aramaic was the official language of the Achaemenid Empire and the main language for most of western Asia before it was replaced by Greek and local Iranian languages. It is believed that Jesus and the first Christians spoke Aramaic.*

*The edicts suggest that Aramaic still existed in Ashoka's time, long after the fall of the Achaemenid Empire. They also reveal the importance of the Greeks in the Afghan region, and testify to the existence of humanitarian values at the time.*

troops and besieged it for six months, leaving only forty people alive. The city later flourished under the rule of Tamerlane's son, Shahrukh. Returning from India, he ordered Ghazni destroyed, leaving behind vast expanses of rubble and turning cultivated fields barren. Irrigation canals and wells were filled with sand upon his departure from the region in 1223. Some of this devastation left permanent scars.

While Buddhism was almost totally dislodged from the region, Islam gradually gained a much stronger foothold and continued to flourish.

By the middle of the 14th century, Mongol rule had lost much of its imperial hold, and the only traces left were the few colonies, such as the Hazaras, that the Mongols had established. Both Marco Polo and Ibn Battuta passed through this region during this era and left records of their observations.

Between 1332 and 1370, this region was ruled independently by the Kurds of Herat until the arrival of Tamerlane, a descendant of Genghis Khan. On his route to India, Tamerlane passed over the Hindu Kush, destroying everything

Genghis Khan, the founder of the Mongol Empire, died in 1227. Following his death, power struggles among ambitious chiefs and princes erupted and intensified until Tamerlane's reign in the late 14th century.

in his path; this destruction is evident to this day in the dry waste of the Helmand Valley. Tamerlane was, however, a patron of the arts, and he also organized administration of his lands, constructed public works, and encouraged commerce and industry, introducing new trade routes. Later on, Tamerlane's favorite son, Shahrukh, kept alive the tradition of patronage to art and culture. He rebuilt Herat, which was devastated by Tamerlane in 1383, and actively encouraged the Persian school of miniature painting. Shah Rukh and his wife Gawharshad were experimental patrons of architecture. They looked into the development of shrines to support Shi'ite communities; for example, through the patronage and restoration of the shrine of Imam Riza at Mashhad. Thus Herat became a great center of Persian art and culture during the 15th and 16th century. Tamerlane's Timurid dynasty lasted about 100 years, during which Afghanistan enjoyed much growth and prosperity.

When Tamerlane's empire shrank, several local chieftains took over different parts of the region. One of them, Bahlol Lodi, captured the throne at Delhi and founded the Lodi dynasty, which lasted for just 75 years. His power, however, encouraged many Afghans to move to India, where they were eventually integrated into the local population.

Babur (whose name means "tiger" in Arabic), a Timurid prince and another descendant of Genghis Khan, set out with a few thousand followers on a journey that ended in the founding of the great Moghul Empire of India at the beginning of the 16th century. Babur had a very special affection for Kabul; finding its scenery and climate delightful, he made the city his capital until 1526, when he moved to Delhi. Delhi's strategic and economic importance made it easier for him to administer his huge empire from there. After making Delhi his capital, he never returned to Kabul during the remainder of his lifetime. Still he asked to be buried in Kabul.

The Moghul armies depended heavily on recruitment among the Afghans of the Sulaiman Mountains. These ethnic groups played a major role in the eventual disintegration of the Moghul Empire. They achieved this by masterfully pitting the Persians and the Moghuls against each other in their struggle to control the strategic areas of the mountain crossroads.

# BIRTH OF THE AFGHAN STATE

For a while, the Ghilzai Pashtuns (or Pashtuns), under the leadership of a general called Mir Wais Khan, overthrew the Persians and took control of a large part of the Persian Empire. However, because of internal disputes and strife, they lost not only Persia but also Kandahar to Nadir Shah, a Turkish warrior from Khorasan. After defeating the Pashtuns near Jalalabad, Nadir Shah marched through the Khyber Pass to Delhi.

Son of a Pashtun chief of the Abdali tribe and a member of the Sadozai group, Ahmad Khan Abdali was a general in Nadir Shah's army. In the skirmishes on the night in 1747 that Nadir Shah was assassinated, Ahmad Khan fought his way out of the Persian camp, seized a convoy carrying treasure (including the now-famous Koh-i-Noor diamond that Nadir Shah had looted from Delhi), and marched to Kandahar.

The Afghans then announced that they no longer owed allegiance to Persia and declared independence under Ahmad Khan, who took on the title of Ahmad Shah, the king of Afghanistan.

Over the next 26 years, Ahmad Shah created a single Afghanistan out of what until then had been a land fragmented into distinctly different regions ruled by diverse foreign powers or local chiefs. He took the title of Durrani, or *Doori Dooraani* (DOO-ri-DOO-RAH-ni), meaning the "Pearl of Pearls."

Ahmad Shah Durrani went on to seize all the territories west of the Indus from Kashmir to the Arabian Sea. In 1761, when he defeated the Mahrattas in India, his empire had reached its zenith. Within 40 years of his death in 1773, Ahmad Shah's great empire fell apart. Bickering and power struggles among his successors led to the downfall of the ruling family. Although his son Timur Shah had 23 sons, he died without naming an heir, and for a quarter of a century after this, the Durrani princes were entangled in a web of intrigue and conspiracy against one another.

When the princes executed the chieftain of the rival Mohamadzais and blinded his eldest son, the latter group rebelled. The dead chieftain's youngest son, Dost Mohammad Khan, then defeated the Durrani ruler near Kabul.

Babur's marble tomb lies in the Gardens of Babur, or Bagh-e Babur, in Kabul. He was a poet of considerable gifts. His prose memoirs, the *Baburnama*, originally written in Turki, were later translated into Farsi and then into English in the 20th century.

## ARRIVAL OF WESTERN POWERS

By this time very little of the Durrani kingdom was left, and when the Sikhs began pressing their claims to Peshawar, Dost Mohammad sought military help from the British. The British in India were moving north at the same time as the Russians were moving south into Central Asia. As only the land in the Hindu Kush remained sandwiched between these Western powers, Afghanistan became a pawn between them. When the British refused to support Afghan claims in the Punjab, Dost Mohammad turned to the czar, or emperor, of Russia for help.

The British invaded Afghanistan, precipitating the First Anglo-Afghan War (1839—42). They captured Kandahar and Ghazni. Dost Mohammad fled, and the British placed Shah Shoja, a puppet monarch, on the throne and garrisoned Kabul. The Afghans rebelled, and the harassed British troops were forced to evacuate Kabul. Although the leaders in Kabul had promised safe passage for the British, this promise carried little weight with the Afghans. The British column was massacred before it could reach Jalalabad, and, according to some reports, only one man survived.

A painting of an English diplomat killed by rebel Afghans during the First Anglo-Afghan War.

Shah Shoja was assassinated by the Afghans, and Dost Mohammad returned to Afghanistan. Before he died in 1863, he managed to unify Afghanistan. Dost Mohammad was subsequently succeeded by his son Sher Ali.

The Russians, having moved their troops to the Afghan border in 1878, sent an uninvited diplomatic mission to Afghanistan. When the British sent a counter-mission, the group was stopped by Afghan border guards. The British demanded an apology. Unappeased by Sher Ali's explanation, they invaded Afghanistan in December 1878, leading to the Second Anglo-Afghan War (1878—1880). Sher Ali fled north, seeking Russian help. He was unsuccessful in his appeal and died at Mazar-i-Sharif in 1879.

After Sher Ali's death the British placed his son, Yaqoob Khan, in charge; he agreed to all of the British demands, including the appointment of a British advisor. The fiercely independent and proud Afghans found

Yaqoob Khan's submission unacceptable. Resentful toward the foreign presence and pressure, they assassinated the British representatives, resulting in the British army's occupation of Kabul and Kandahar. Yaqoob Khan abdicated and fled to India.

The attacks by the Afghans against the British, however, did not cease. In 1880 the British eventually relinquished Afghanistan to emir Abdur Rahman, a grandson of Dost Mohammad, but continued to manage Afghanistan's foreign affairs. The Durand Line was defined to mark the boundary between British India and Afghanistan. The line cut through the region inhabited by the Pashtuns and has been a source of contention ever since. Abdur Rahman was forced to accept the Wakhan Corridor (the remote region covered by the Pamir range) from the British as part of Afghanistan, in order to create a buffer between Russia and British India. Reluctantly he took on the responsibility of controlling the Kyrgyz outlaws located in the Wakhan.

## MOVES TOWARD MODERNIZATION

Abdur Rahman's first task was to unite the country—he tried to reduce the power of the various groups by centralizing power in the government. Besides establishing strong control over these factions, the determined leader implemented a string of reforms to modernize the country. His son, Habibullah Khan, introduced Western medicine, abolished slavery, and founded colleges based on those in Europe.

During World War I, Afghanistan maintained its neutrality despite pressure from its neighbors. When Habibullah was assassinated, his son Amanullah Khan assumed control. To gain complete independence from the British, Amanullah launched a surprise attack on British troops in India, starting the Third Anglo-Afghan War (1919—1921). In the peace treaty signed in Rawalpindi in 1921, Britain agreed not to interfere in Afghanistan's foreign policy and relations.

Amanullah angered the conservative families and the mullahs, or Muslim clerics, by introducing drastic reforms to modernize Afghanistan. He abolished the purdah, or the mandatory face-concealing veil for women,

Abdur Rahman was emir of Afghanistan from 1880 to 1901.

Ahmad Shah made Kandahar the capital of his empire. In 1776, three years after his death, the capital was moved to Kabul by his son Timur Shah.

opened coeducational schools, introduced Western dress, and started a program to educate the nomads.

Bitter resentment against modernization grew and, in 1928, many Afghan tribes and leaders revolted, leading to Amanullah's abdication, the following year. After nine months of chaos, the great-grandson of one of Dost Mohammad's brothers, Mohammad Nadir Khan, emerged. An assembly of chiefs proclaimed him Nadir Shah, the next king of Afghanistan.

Mohammad Nadir Khan, or Nadir Shah, based his administration on orthodox Islamic law and set up the *Loya Jirga*, or Grand Assembly, with all Afghan groups represented. From it the National Council was formed. An upper house consisting of intellectuals was also created. Political parties, however, were not allowed to operate. Mohammad Nadir Khan abolished some of the reforms of Amanullah that had angered the conservative elements, and women were returned to the purdah. When Mohammad Nadir Khan was assassinated in 1933, his son Mohammed Zahir Shah was proclaimed king. During World War II, the new king managed to maintain the country's neutrality and Afghanistan emerged relatively unscathed from the war. The country also prospered under the reforms of Zahir Shah. In 1953 Mohammad Daud Khan, Zahir Shah's cousin, became prime minister. He secured aid from the Soviet Union and began planning to modernize the country. His term as prime minister ended with his resignation in 1963.

Zahir Shah signed a new democratic constitution into law in 1964, with a fully elected lower house and a partly elected upper house. Political parties were still not allowed to operate. In 1973, when the country was devastated and ravaged by a spate of natural disasters, Daud reappeared and overthrew the monarchy of Mohammed Zahir Shah in a bloodless coup, or a coup d'état. Afghanistan was subsequently declared a republic with Daud as prime minister.

In 1978 Daud was killed in a coup after attempting to crack down on his political foes. This came to be known as the Saur Revolution. Leaders of the communist People's Democratic Party of Afghanistan (PDPA) subsequently assumed control of the country. Nur Mohammad Taraki became the president of the Revolutionary Council and the prime minister of Afghanistan. Babrak Karmal was chosen to be Afghanistan's deputy prime minister.

The PDPA was divided into two factions: the People's (Khalq) Party, led by Hafizullah Amin and Taraki, and the more moderate Banner (Parcham) Party, led by Karmal. These two political groups had reunited in an uneasy coalition before the coup, but old ideological and ethnic conflicts between the factions soon resurfaced. The new government had little popular support and forged close ties with the Soviet Union. Ruthless purges of all domestic opposition took place and extensive land and social reforms were undertaken. These reforms were hugely unpopular with the devoutly Muslim and anticommunist populace. Thousands of people were killed or imprisoned without trial, and sweeping land reforms and radical social changes were decreed. The black, red, and green Islamic flag was replaced by a red communist one.

Only ruins remain of the tomb of Mohammad Nadir Khan, or Nadir Shah, in Kabul. Mohammad Nadir Khan was assassinated in 1933.

## SOVIET INVASION

Armed resistance to the communist regime, which soon developed into guerrilla warfare, mounted during the winter of 1978. Desertion by Afghan soldiers grew as Soviet advisors tightened their hold over the army, and a network of guerrilla training camps was developed in Pakistan and Iran.

In October 1979 Hafizullah Amin had Taraki killed when it became clear that Taraki, with Soviet backing, was plotting to eliminate him. President Amin's own days, however, were numbered. On Christmas Eve, 1979, Soviet troops began landing at the Kabul airport, launching an invasion of Afghanistan. Afghan troops were no match for the well-armed Soviets. Amin was killed after the presidential palace in Kabul came under siege, and Babrak Karmal was installed as president of the Democratic Republic of Afghanistan by the Soviet Union.

Insurgencies among both tribal and urban groups arose against the government. The Muslim groups united in a mujahideen resistance movement and waged a fierce guerrilla war financed by Pakistan and the United States. The rebellion grew, spreading to all parts of the country. The Soviets, despite their vastly superior arms and resources, were unable to defeat the mountain-based rebels. The Afghan War settled down into a stalemate, with more than 100,000 Soviet troops controlling the larger towns and cities, and the mujahideen moving with relative freedom through the more difficult terrain of the countryside. Soviet troops tried a variety of tactics to crush the insurgency, but the guerrillas eluded them. The Soviets tried to eliminate the mujahideen's civilian support by depopulating and bombing the rural areas. By 1982 about 3 million Afghans had fled to Pakistan and another 1.5 million to Iran. The United States, adversaries of the Soviet Union, supplied the Afghans with shoulder-fired aircraft missiles and the mujahideen were eventually able to neutralize Soviet air power.

When Mikhail Gorbachev came to power in the Soviet Union in 1985, he began moves to end his country's intervention in Afghanistan. The war was unpopular with the Soviet public and its costs placed a heavy burden on the Soviet economy. It was also damaging to the Soviet Union's relations with other Muslim countries and detrimental to its political interests.

In 1986 Karmal was replaced by the communist regime of Najibullah. In April 1988 a ceasefire was declared after Afghanistan, Pakistan, the Soviet Union, and the United States concluded a series of agreements in Geneva for a Soviet troop withdrawal. The withdrawal began in May 1988 and was completed in February 1989, when Afghanistan returned to nonaligned status, leaving the cities in the hands of a pro-Moscow government and

A Russian tank and other Soviet military vehicles passing through a main road in Kabul. By the year 1988 there were some 115,000 Soviet troops stationed in Afghanistan. Many countries, including the United States, boycotted the 1980 Summer Olympic Games in Moscow in protest against the Soviet invasion.

the countryside in the hands of the mujahideen. Both the Soviet Union and the United States, however, continued to send weapons into Afghanistan. The mujahideen were soon armed with increasingly sophisticated weapons.

The communist regime of Najibullah survived another three years before being overthrown by the mujahideen in April 1992. Najibullah, unable to flee Kabul, took refuge at the United Nations compound. Rival mujahideen leaders and their parties continued struggling for supremacy.

## CIVIL WAR

General Abdul Rashid Dostum, an Uzbek militia leader, defected to the mujahideen units of Ahmad Shah Masood, a Tajik. In April 1992 fighting erupted between them, the Hizbi Islami under the command of Gulbuddin Hekmatyar, and the Hizbi Wahdat of the Shi'a Hazaras. The Islamic state of Afghanistan was established, but the fighting continued.

## THE TALIBAN

In 1994 a small band of former mujahideen, led by a minor commander named Mullah Muhammad Omar, rose up and overthrew the warlord in Kandahar and took control of the province. The Afghan people were weary of the constant fighting among the many mujahideen factions, and supported the Taliban initially. At first they were for neutralizing and disbanding many of the violent, mercenary militias that had formed throughout Afghanistan. Many from the rank and file of the mujahideen joined them when they started to occupy the rest of the country.

The Pakistani military also encouraged thousands of Afghan and Pakistani students from the religious schools, or madrasahs, and refugee camps throughout Pakistan across the border to join Mullah Omar's partisans. These new recruits were called Taliban, or religious students; hence the name of this movement.

A Taliban propaganda poster featuring Osama bin Laden in an Al-Qaeda classroom in Zhawar Kili. Osama bin Laden was the suspected mastermind of the terrorist attacks in 2001. The subsequent hunt for Osama led to the collapse of the Taliban regime and the opening of a new chapter in Afghan experience.

By September 1996 they occupied Kabul, and by 1998 they were in control of 90 percent of the country. The remaining opposition was confined to the northeast and the Panjshir Valley. The warlords there formed the Northern Alliance, a coalition of various Afghan factions fighting the Taliban.

The Taliban established a regime of severe religious extremism and were ruthless in imposing their laws. The laws governing women were extremely stringent. Punishment was cruel and swift. Disobedience could mean the death penalty. Criminals were publicly executed and the education of women was prohibited. Religious minorities, such as the Shi'a Hazaras, were subjected to severe atrocities. Many were slaughtered. The group is known for having provided safe haven to Al-Qaeda and its leader, Osama bin Laden.

Al-Qaeda, an international terrorist network that was an ally of the Taliban and had its headquarters and training centers in Afghanistan, was held responsible for the August 1998 bombings of the United States embassies in Nairobi, Kenya, and in Dar-es-Salaam, Tanzania. The United States, in retaliation, launched a missile attack on Al-Qaeda terrorist training camps located in southeastern Afghanistan.

## A NEW BEGINNING AFTER THE TALIBAN

Osama bin Laden was suspected of being Al-Qaeda's top leader and of masterminding the attacks on the Twin Towers of the World Trade Center in New York and the Pentagon in Washington, D.C., which occurred on September 11, 2001.

The Taliban, however, refused to hand over Osama bin Laden to the United States. In October 2001 the United States, together with the antiterrorist coalition, launched a military campaign targeting key terrorist facilities and political and financial centers. In 2001 a United States led an invasion to drive the Taliban from power. The Taliban disintegrated, and on November 13, 2001, lost control of Kabul. Although the Taliban has been out of power for several years, it remains resilient in the region. The anti-Taliban factions, sponsored by the UN, met in Bonn, Germany. The Bonn Agreement paved the way for the development of a new Afghanistan. An interim government called the Transitional Islamic State of Afghanistan (TISA) was set up on December 7, 2001. Hamid Karzai, a Pashtun leader, was appointed by the UN-led coalition to head this government. With the help of the international community, Afghanistan thus began its move toward establishing peace, democracy, and political and economic stability. It has since embarked on ambitious efforts in national reconstruction and change. One of the TISA's achievements was to draft a constitution that was ratified by a *loya jirga* on January 4, 2004. In December 2004 the country was renamed the Islamic Republic of Afghanistan.

The first national democratic presidential election was held in October 2005, and more than 8 million Afghans, 41 percent of whom were women, voted. Hamid Karzai won the election and was inaugurated as president. Karzai was re-elected in 2009 for another five-year term.

## INTERNET LINKS

**www.asia.si.edu/explore/shahnama/firdawsi.asp**

This website of the Smithsonian Institution contains information about the poet Firdawsi and his epic poem "Shahnama."

**www.afghanan.net/afghanistan/ghorids.htm**

This website is devoted to Afghanistan's history, with many links to specific periods and rulers.

**http://ngm.nationalgeographic.com/2008/02/afghanistan-hazara/phil-zabriskie-text/2**

Article within *National Geographic* online magazine about the Hazara people, how they are sometimes considered outsiders, and why it is thought that they are descended from Genghis Khan's Mongolian soldiers.

Osama bin Laden, believed to have ordered the attacks on New York and Washington that resulted in the deaths of thousands of innocent civilians, had been top of the United States' "Most Wanted" list since 2001. In May 2011 he was found inside a compound near Islamabad in Pakistan and shot dead in an operation based on U.S. intelligence.

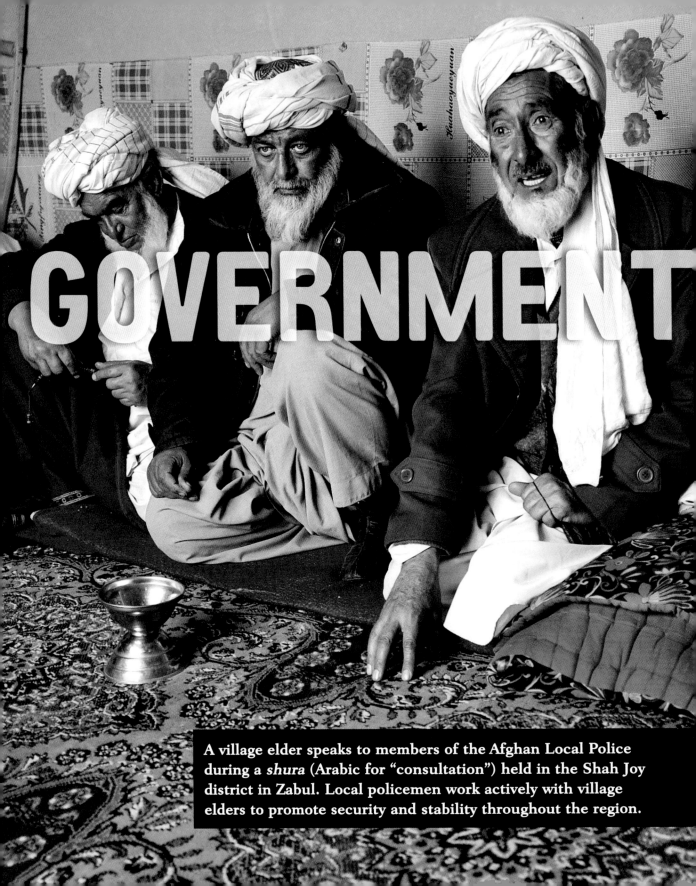

# GOVERNMENT

A village elder speaks to members of the Afghan Local Police during a *shura* (Arabic for "consultation") held in the Shah Joy district in Zabul. Local policemen work actively with village elders to promote security and stability throughout the region.

**3**

THE GOVERNMENT OF AFGHANISTAN has undergone several radical changes in the last two decades of the 20th century and first few years of the new millennium. In 1973 the constitutional monarchy of Zahir Shah was overthrown by Daud Khan and Afghanistan was declared a republic.

Daud's efforts to bring about social, political, and economic stability failed. Communism took a foothold in 1978 after Daud was killed in a coup and the communist PDPA triumphed. In 1992 Najibullah's Soviet-backed regime collapsed, and the Islamic State of Afghanistan was proclaimed.

On New Year's Day in 1994 hostilities again broke out in Kabul and the northern provinces as rival mujahideen groups jostled for power. The power struggle among the mujahideen factions intensified.

In late 1996 the Taliban, a powerful fundamentalist Islamist militia, gained control over most of Afghanistan despite the opposing forces of the Northern Alliance—a coalition of the Uzbeks, Tajiks, and Hazaras of northern Afghanistan.

The Taliban regime was harsh and oppressive, and it played host to certain Muslim extremists. It remained largely unrecognized in the international community, and its terrorist links led to the implementation of strict economic sanctions against the repressed country by the United States and its Western counterparts.

After the September 11, 2001, terrorist attacks, the Taliban were dealt a devastating blow in a retaliatory attack from the United States and its antiterrorist partners. In early December that same year,

Historically, the government of Afghanistan has been very unstable with a large number of power struggles, coups, and unstable transfers of power. The country has been governed by many systems. It has been a monarchy, republic, theocracy, dictatorship, and a pro-communist state. Currently Afghanistan is an Islamic republic. In 2004 Afghanistan held its first national democratic presidential elections.

President Hamid Karzai leads the country's pursuit of change and stability.

Hamid Karzai assumed chairmanship of an interim government put in place after the Bonn Agreement was reached by members of the international community who were committed to helping Afghanistan on its path toward democracy and national transformation.

At the *loya jirga*, or Grand Assembly, held in mid-June of 2002, a constitution was drawn up. This was ratified at the constitutional *loya jirga* on January 4, 2004. More than 8 million Afghans, eager to rebuild their nation after decades of conflict and deprivation, voted in the presidential election held on October 9, 2004. Hamid Karzai won a 55.4 percent majority of the votes and was inaugurated as president of the Islamic Republic of Afghanistan, ending the transitional government.

The country's landmark parliamentary elections for the *Wolesi Jirga* (woo-LAW-si jorhr-GA), or House of the People, and the local councils were conducted on September 18, 2005. On November 12, 2005, after much local and international speculation and anticipation, the results of the parliamentary polls were finalized. The winning candidates, or new parliamentarians, belong to and are representative of the various factions of Afghan national life.

Since the fall of the Taliban regime, destabilizing factors within the country have continued and include activities by the Taliban and other insurgents and Al-Qaeda. In October 2011 a Taliban suicide bomber rammed a vehicle loaded with explosives into an armored North Atlantic Treaty Organization (NATO) bus in Kabul and killed 17 people, including 12 Americans. The Taliban and related groups have staged many similar attacks in an apparent campaign to weaken confidence in the Afghan government ahead of a 2014 deadline for the United States and other NATO countries to withdraw their troops. Even so the government's authority is growing and there is an optimistic sentiment that the country's new democratic inclination will help in the establishment of a common national identity and the pursuit of peace and change.

The Afghan army collapsed in 1992 and disintegrated into factional groups after President Najibullah was ousted. Its equipment then included about 1,200 battle tanks.

## THE PRESIDENT

According to the constitution of 2004, the president is elected by popular vote to a term of five years. He must be over 40 years of age, a Muslim, and a citizen.

The president is the head of state and government, and commander in chief of the armed forces. He appoints members of his cabinet, military and police personnel, and provincial governors. These appointments have to be approved by the parliament. His tenure is limited to two terms only. There are two vice presidents. The vice presidents are appointed by the president and they act in accordance with the provisions of the constitution during the absence, resignation, and or death of the president.

In 2009 the second national democratic presidential elections were held. Hamid Karzai's main competitor Abdullah Abdullah forced a presidential run-off to be scheduled but then withdrew. Officials on the Independent Election Commission (IEC) declared Hamid Karzai president of Afghanistan for another five-year term. The first vice president is Mohammad Qasim Fahim and the second vice president is Abdul Karim Khalili.

The 25 ministers in the cabinet are appointed by the president and approved by the National Assembly.

An Afghan woman gets to exercise her right to vote at the 2010 parliamentary elections. Her participation is symbolic of the emancipation of Afghan women after the defeat of the Taliban.

## THE LEGISLATIVE BODY

The *Meli Shura* (National Assembly) is the two-chambered parliament that is made up of the lower house, *Wolesi Jirga*, or House of the People, and the upper house, *Meshrano Jirga*, or House of the Elders.

## THE *WOLESI JIRGA*

The *Wolesi Jirga* consists of no more than 250 members who are elected for a term of five years. Each province is represented in proportion to its population, similar to the U.S. House of Representatives. The number of seats for women must be at least twice the number of provinces.

In September 2005 an election was held for the *Wolesi Jirga* of Afghanistan's new bicameral National Assembly and for the country's 34 provincial councils. There were 12.5 million registered voters, and the turnout was about 53 percent of the population. The first democratically elected National Assembly since 1969 was inaugurated in December 2005.

## THE *MESHRANO JIRGA*

The *Meshrano Jirga* consists of 102 seats. One-third of the members are elected from the provincial councils, and they serve for four years. Another third are elected from local district councils of each province and serve for three years. Of the last third, appointed by the president, half must be women, with at least two from the nomadic Kuchis, and two representatives of the disabled. These will serve for five years.

## THE JUDICIAL SYSTEM

The judicial system consists of the *Stera Mahkama*, or the Supreme Court, and subordinate High Courts and Appeals Courts. The *Stera Mahkama* has nine judges appointed by the president with approval from the *Wolesi Jirga* for a term of 10 years. The judges should be above 40 years of age and are not to be affiliated with any political party. They should hold a degree in law or Islamic jurisprudence. The *Stera Mahkama* has the power to judge and assess the constitutionality of all laws in the country. There is also a minister of justice and a separate Afghan Human Rights Commission established by the Bonn Agreement and responsible for investigating human rights abuses and war crimes.

According to the constitution, no law should be contrary to Islamic principles. The state is to create a prosperous and progressive society, based on social justice and the protection of human rights and dignity. It is to be democratic and promote unity and equality among the various ethnic groups. The state should abide by the UN Charter, commit to all international treaties and conventions signed by the country, and observe the guidelines in the Universal Declaration of Human Rights.

## LOYA JIRGA

The *loya jirga*, or grand assembly, is the traditional method Afghans have used throughout history to solve their political crises. A *loya jirga* refers to a national gathering to discuss important issues of a national scale. This traditional method derives from the Islamic / Arab *shura* (consultative assembly) as well as from pre-Islamic local practices. It is traditionally the only political process honored and accepted by all ethnic and religious groups. It is convened only on occasions to decide on matters concerning the country's independence, national sovereignty, and territorial integrity. It amends provisions of the constitution and has the power to prosecute the president. It includes members of the National Assembly and the chairpersons of the district and provisional councils.

The word *jirga*, meaning "a circle of people," is used in Afghanistan to cover various kinds of gatherings where the people present will consult and discuss the relevant issue. Local and tribal *jirgas* are often held to settle everyday disputes among tribes or individuals.

## INTERNET LINKS

**www.biography.com/people/hamid-karzai-537356?page=1**

This is a biography of Afghanistan's first president, Hamid Karzai.

**www.afghan-web.com/anthem/**

This website contains detailed information on Afghanistan. There is a page dedicated to the national anthem where you can follow a link to listen to the anthem.

**www.bu.edu/aias/**

The American Institute of Afghanistan Studies (AIAS) is a private, non-profit organization run by scholars to promote the study of the culture, society, land, languages, health, peoples, and history of Afghanistan.

After the collapse of the Taliban regime, the internal security of the country was found to be in shambles. The military and police lacked professional training, guidelines, and rules by which to maintain law and order. They served different factions and were corrupt. The Afghan National Army was soon formed and trained with the help of international forces and trainers in a bid to help the newly democratized country fend for itself eventually.

# ECONOMY

Like this farmer in Kushk-i Kuhna, Herat, many Afghan farmers plow their fields with oxen, as they cannot afford modern machinery and have no access to electricity.

# 4

LANDLOCKED AND DEVASTATED by decades of political chaos, violence, and war, Afghanistan is highly dependent on foreign assistance in its reconstruction and rebuilding efforts.

A report published by the UN from the Office of the High Commissioner for Human Rights (OHCHR) in 2010 stated that about 9 million Afghans—36 percent of the population—live in absolute poverty and a further 37 percent of the population lives only slightly above the poverty line.

Only 23 percent of the population has access to safe drinking water. About 80 percent of the Afghan population still resided in rural and undeveloped areas in 2010, and little has been done since to improve their living conditions. It is estimated that about 42.3 percent of the population is under 14 years of age. Average life expectancy is 49 years for men and 52 for women. Along with a high infant mortality rate, Afghanistan suffers from one of the highest levels of maternal mortality in the world, with 1,200 deaths per 100,000 live births. More than half of children under the age of five are malnourished and suffer from micronutrient deficiencies in iodine and iron.

In January 2002 the International Conference on Reconstruction Assistance to Afghanistan was held in Tokyo. Sixty-one countries and twenty-one international organizations attended, and $4.5 billion was pledged over a five-year period toward development in Afghanistan.

After the fall of the oppressive Taliban regime, four years of severe drought, and the generous outpouring of international assistance of $8.4 billion by 2005, the economy of Afghanistan has improved considerably. Foreign aid to Afghanistan continues as the United States and other nations have pledged $15 billion to aid the country through 2015.

Afghanistan is landlocked, extremely poor, and highly dependent on foreign aid. The economy has been affected by the perilous security and political situation that overshadows activity in the country, but it is slowly recovering from decades of conflict and war. The economy has improved significantly since the fall of the Taliban in 2001 primarily because of the recovery of the agricultural sector, service sector growth, and international economic assistance.

Between 2002 and 2010 U.S. assistance to Afghanistan totaled $51.8 billion. Yet, despite the progress made in recent years, Afghanistan still remains among the poorest countries of the world.

The country faces the challenges of stabilizing and strengthening its economy and national security, eradicating the opium trade and corruption, and grappling with unprecedented population pressure in the cities, as more displaced Afghans return.

## AGRICULTURE

Afghanistan's economy is predominantly agricultural, and the sector employs about 78.6 percent of the active workforce, but unemployment is at least 35 percent. The country's main products are opium, hashish, wheat, rice, barley, fruits, nuts, vegetables, wool, cotton, lamb, and sheepskins. Only 12 percent of its land area is arable and suitable for cultivation. Of that, only 0.21 percent is permanently cultivated. Although harvests were abundant during the good times, the endless conflict, hardships, oppression, and natural devastation of the last two decades of the 20th century—war against the Soviet Union, the subsequent civil war, and a severe drought that lasted four years—impoverished and laid bare many parts of the country. Afghanistan is also prone to natural disasters, such as earthquakes, flooding, landslides, and avalanches. Earthquakes are frequent. It is estimated that between 1980 and 2010 about 20,000 people were killed and more than 6 million people were adversely affected by natural disasters. The resultant exodus to nearby Iran and Pakistan, as well as increasing migration to urban areas, has led to a shortage of labor in the fields and further worsened the fall in agricultural production. Millions of Afghans to this day remain dependent on international food aid.

Opium accounts for 9 percent of Afghanistan's gross domestic product (GDP), or national revenue, according to UN estimates. Easy to cultivate, process, and transport, opium has become a quick source of income to the impoverished Afghan. Afghanistan is the world's leading opium supplier, responsible for 90 percent of the global supply. The latest Afghanistan Opium Survey by the UN Office of Drugs and Crime found that opium cultivation rose by 7 percent in 2011 compared with the previous year. Insecurity and the high market value make it difficult to stop the farmers from growing the crop, despite improved eradication efforts.

In 2009 Afghanistan harvested its biggest wheat crop since the Department of Agriculture started keeping records for the country. Certified wheat seeds are distributed to farmers in rain-fed areas where other crops cannot be planted, but in irrigated areas wheat cultivation is not actively encouraged because it is not a lucrative crop. Only about a third of farmland in Afghanistan is irrigated. The rest is only suitable for rain-fed wheat cultivation. A farmer can earn $200 to $250 per acre of wheat, but the same land area could yield as much as $25,000, if saffron is cultivated or $13,000, if almonds are grown.

A cotton merchant in Herat.

Through a project partially financed by Germany, the Food and Agriculture Organization of the UN (FAO) rehabilitated Afghanistan's only sugar factory in Baghlan, which had ceased operating in the 1970s. In 2005 the New Baghlan Sugar Company was established, but progress was halted for several months during parliamentary elections when foreign personnel working on the installation of equipment received death threats. In 2006 the first sugar was produced. In 2007 the factory was officially inaugurated, but on the day of the inauguration it became the subject of a suicide attack and approximately 70 people were killed, including children who were participating in the ceremony. After four years in operation the enterprise has failed, primarily because it was never possible to provide the factory with enough of the raw material—sugar beets—for processing.

Long before cotton mills were built, raw cotton had been an important export for Afghanistan. Cotton has gained much economic importance, providing raw materials to the growing number of mills that have been repaired and refurbished. In 2010 the Lashkar Gah cotton factory, which had been built by the British government in the 1960s, was reopened under the ownership of the Islamic Republic of Afghanistan with no help from the coalition forces. This and other renovated mills have allowed hundreds of farmers to bring their cotton to be processed far more efficiently than had previously been possible. Another significant agricultural activity is fruit farming, which is concentrated mainly in the Kabul and Arghandab valleys. Many of the farms there were destroyed, however, during the turbulent years of warfare. In January 2011 Afghan villagers returned to their village of Tarook Kalacha, which they had been forced to leave. Fierce fighting had broken out in the Arghandab River Valley when U.S. troops pushed into Taliban territory. The Taliban fighters eventually left the area and the fighting was stopped, but it was so full of homemade land mines—what the U.S. military call IEDs— that the only way that the village could be saved was to demolish it with airstrikes. Not only were the houses completely destroyed, but so were the surrounding pomegranate orchards, vineyards, and mulberry tree groves. Reconstruction is under way, and the villagers are to be compensated for the houses and lost fruit harvest.

In the valleys, orchards potentially yield apples, pears, peaches, quinces, apricots, plums, cherries, pomegranates, and many varieties of grapes and melons. Nuts such as almonds, pistachios, and walnuts also grow well and, together with fresh fruits and vegetables, are important exports. The main markets are India and Pakistan. Coffee is also exported.

Developing new markets for Afghanistan's fresh fruit is vitally important for the development of the agricultural sector, both to reassure farmers that there is a viable market for their produce, and to increase job opportunities. In 2011 five Afghan companies attended the opening of the India Fresh Fruit Trade Office, looking for ways to expand their export sales. The trade office put the fruit traders in touch with 19 new Indian buyers. Although India has a huge and profitable fresh fruit market of its own, Afghan produce is of a good quality and attracts a high price because it is harvested at a different time of year. Just a week after these meetings, one of the traders exported its first shipment of apricots to New Delhi. In addition to the Indian market, Afghan traders are selling fruit to the United Arab Emirates, Europe, and Canada.

Primitive farming methods are still employed. Plowing is often done with oxen and wooden plows, seeds are not scientifically selected, and land is not properly fertilized. Harvesting is performed manually. The grains are then milled by hand or sent to local mills. The farmers barter their produce in return for meager quantities of cloth, sugar, tea, and other basic necessities.

Noncommissioned officers have been sent to Afghanistan from the United States as Agribusiness Development Teams. In civilian life these men work in agriculture or agribusiness. They have real expertise in farming, and they are in Afghanistan to help the Afghan farmers improve their farming techniques, and thereby their production. Afghan farmers typically broadcast seed; it is literally scattered by hand. Planting in straight rows is more time-consuming, but it makes the land easier to weed, enables the use of tools, and most important, increases the yield. Afghan farmers are encouraged to keep better records so that they will be able to assess how much wheat needs how much fertilizer. Gradually farming methods are improving. Livestock rearing is the second most important occupation. The wool, skins, and meat of Karakul sheep are important export commodities. Karakul wool is valued all over the world for its superior quality. It is popular in the United States for making superior-grade Persian lamb coats. Other varieties of sheep are also raised. Cattle provide dairy products. Horses, camels, and donkeys are all used for transport and travel. Goats and chickens are valued sources of food.

The Horticulture and Livestock Project was initiated in 2006 with a budget donated by the World Bank. The aim of the project is to improve the livelihood of rural households through stimulating production and productivity of livestock. Farmers are trained in improved agricultural techniques and both men and women are trained in various associated fields of the agricultural and horticultural industries, including marketing. A liquid nitrogen plant has been installed and the plant operators trained. Twelve thousand women have been selected and organized into groups of 50 for training as poultry keepers. They each received 15 vaccinated layer pullets and 165.3 pounds (75 kilograms) of feed. This project is ongoing as it is recognized that agriculture is the backbone of the Afghanistan economy.

Nomads such as the Kuchis have roamed the land with their herds for centuries. However, much of their pastureland is now riddled with land mines and unexploded bombs from the recent warfare. Traditionally nomadic, many Kuchis have settled in northwest Afghanistan in an area that was traditionally occupied by the Uzbeks and Tajiks. Nowadays only a few thousand Kuchis follow their traditional livelihood of nomadic herding. Others have become farmers, settled in cities, or emigrated to other countries.

New iodized salt plants have been built in Afghanistan since 2003 and now have the capacity to meet the country's requirements. Lack of iodine in the diet can cause a number of adverse medical conditions, such as goiter and stunted growth. As more than 70 percent of women and school-age children are iodine deficient, the Ministry of Public Health and UNICEF have launched a campaign to promote adding iodine to the diet through the use of iodized salt.

## FOREIGN TRADE

Afghanistan's main export partners are Pakistan, India, the United States, and the Netherlands. Imports come mainly from Pakistan, India, the United States, Germany, and Russia.

The country's main legal exports are fruits and nuts, handwoven carpets, leather and furs, cotton and wool, and semiprecious and precious gemstones. It imports capital goods (such as heavy machinery), agriculture supplies, rice, wheat, textiles, and petroleum products.

Carpet weavers at work in Herat. Carpets are an important source of income for Afghans. The international demand for handmade Afghan carpets is still strong and expected to grow given the country's gradually improving infrastructure and expanding trade routes.

## HANDICRAFTS AND INDUSTRY

The largest industries by value of annual output are the small-scale production of textiles, soap, furniture, shoes, fertilizer, apparel, food products, nonalcoholic beverages, mineral water, cement, handwoven carpets, natural gas, coal, and copper. Every village has traditional small industries, including woodworking, leather crafting, basket weaving, pottery, tile molding, and the hand milling of grains. Metalwork is done in small shops throughout the country, using imported sheets of iron. It is in the towns that agricultural implements, such as plows, spades, pickaxes, and utensils and knives for domestic use are manufactured. Coppersmiths fashion pots, trays, and jugs—those produced in Badakhshan and Kandahar are beautifully patterned with intricate designs.

Afghanistan is also famous for its carpets. The wool and dyes are prepared locally, and the carpets are handwoven. Carpet names were traditionally either specifically identified with particular locations such as Bokhara or used to describe particular designs such as Waziri. Since the 1960s labels have been applied fairly indiscriminately. There was a time when Daulatabad in Faryab did produce especially fine carpets and as a result the name began to be used widely (even for those carpets not produced in Daulatabad) to confer an aura of quality. Now Daulatabad has all but disappeared from the quality carpet

# THE ART OF CARPET WEAVING

*The art of carpet weaving is highly traditional, and the majority of patterns are jealously guarded family secrets handed down from one generation to the next. The weaving is done mostly by young girls and women, except in Turkoman, where men also weave. The finest carpets are woven from the hand-spun wool of the Karakul sheep. This has largely been replaced by machine-spun wool. Fine wool carpets may have as many as 355 knots to a square inch (55 knots to the square cm), whereas a coarse carpet only has 129 to 194 knots per square inch (20 to 30 knots per square cm). Carpet weaving is a lengthy and physically difficult process. The finest work requires four workers, who take three months to complete a rug of 6.6 square yards (5.5 square m).*

map. Carpet production has traditionally been a home-based operation, and the weaving is usually carried out by women. Prior to 1978 weavers were not often brought together into a factory to work under supervision on hand-knotted carpets. As a result of the influx of refugees in to the towns and cities it is increasingly common for weavers to work under contract to traders.

Silk weaving of outstanding texture is made in Herat and the Nangarhar Province. However, the traditional craft of silk weaving is undergoing a transformation because cheaper, synthetic silk from Pakistan is replacing natural fibers even though the equality of the finished product is not as good. The demand for pure silk products has decreased in proportion to an increase in price of natural threads. Of the 300 silk weaving looms in Herat city only 12 use pure silk. The major products of Herat silk weaving industries include shawls, scarves, turbans, and fabric. Silk is a shiny, hard, and tense thread which is produced by the silkworm. The silkworm farmers are hoping for government support so that the art of silkworm farming can be revived and made economically viable.

Sheepskin coats of the best quality are made at Ghazni. Silversmiths and goldsmiths all over the country produce jewelry using centuries-old techniques. Precious and semiprecious stones such as lapis lazuli, emeralds, rubies, kunzite, and tourmaline are mined in Afghanistan and used in traditional jewelry.

*Posteens are goat, sheep, or lambskin vests and overcoats worn with the fleece turned inward and the skin facing outward. The best posteens (poss-TEENS) are made from the pelts of lambs. They are embroidered, usually in the favorite color combination of blue, black, orange, and yellow. The posteen is a traditional item of clothing, more frequently worn by elderly or middle-aged men.*

*Women who live in urban areas and villages near towns embroider posteens and other articles of clothing, including the skullcaps worn under turbans, vests, and burkas or* chadaris, *garments worn by women outdoors that cover the face and body. Color combinations and designs vary in different parts of the country.*

## MINING

Afghanistan has potentially rich, varied, and extensive mineral resources. From a global perspective Afghanistan is still relatively unexplored and the potential to discover further copper and other mineral deposits is high. Many sites need further exploration. Its main base metallic mineral deposit is copper, of which there are already more than 300 documented deposits. Other metals and minerals found in Afghanistan include chrome, copper, lead, zinc, uranium, manganese, asbestos, gold, silver, iron, sulfur, mica, nickel, slate, halite, talc, and salt. The rare metals beryllium, lithium, tantalum, and niobium, all of which are used in the aircraft industry, have been identified in Afghanistan but it has yet to be ascertained that mining them is economically viable. Lapis lazuli, emerald, ruby, aquamarine, amethyst, topaz, tourmaline, jade, and quartz are just some of the precious and semiprecious gems that have been discovered. Besides these, large deposits of granite, marble, alabaster, gypsum, clay for making china, and soapstone have also been found.

A copper processing plant near Kabul provides 20 percent of the country's needs. The country's huge deposits of iron ore, as well as most other mineral resources, are largely undeveloped because of the lack of adequate infrastructure, including transportation.

Afghanistan is the world's leading producer of lapis lazuli from the Sary-Sang mine in Badakhshan Province. This deep blue semiprecious gem has been mined in Afghanistan for at least 6,000 years. Most operations today are small-scale, but there is potential for the development of a significant precious stone mining industry in Afghanistan.

Afghanistan has moderate to potentially abundant resources of coal but most deposits are currently inaccessible or relatively deep. The reserves are mostly undeveloped. Historically coal has been used as the main source of household fuel, but it has also been used on an industrial scale to power small industries such as textiles, manufacturing, and cement production. The main factors that inhibit the widespread use of coal in Afghanistan are the rugged terrain and lack of transportation networks.

Development of Afghanistan's oil and natural gas reserves is essential to the country's economic development. Recent estimates by the U.S. Geological Survey suggest that northern Afghanistan, especially in the northeast Afghan-Tajikistan Basin, holds up to 1.8 billion barrels of oil. State-owned China National Petroleum Corp (CNPC) was given approval by the Afghan government to sign the joint-venture deal with the diversified Afghan company, the Watan Group, to lead the exploration for oil in three fields in the Kashkari, Bazarkhami, and Zamarudsay basins. Located in the northern provinces of Sar-e Pul and Faryab, they are estimated to hold around 87 million barrels of oil—small on a global scale, but significantly profitable for Kabul.

The most important resource of Afghanistan is natural gas. Development of the Sheberghan gas fields has long been considered essential to the region's economic growth. According to a 2010 USAID report, between 1959 and the 1980s, 144 gas wells were drilled in the three Sheberghan gas fields. With 70 completed production wells nearly 2,260 billion cubic feet (64 billion cubic meters) of gas was produced. It is estimated that the three fields hold an additional 1,200 billion cubic feet (34 billion cubic meters) of gas in the produced reservoirs. In 2011 an agreement was signed between the Overseas Private Investment Corporation (OPIC), the U.S. government's development finance institution, the U.S. Agency for International Development (USAID), and the government of Afghanistan to begin a 200-megawatt project. The project will build and operate a gas-fired power plant in the area of the three natural gas fields in Sheberghan. The electricity produced by the plant will provide a significant proportion of power for Afghanistan's industrial northern region.

## TOURISM

Another source of foreign revenue, tourism, had almost completely disappeared in the last two decades of the 20th century. In the past, Kabul used to be a popular stopover for backpackers, and Afghanistan was known for its dramatic mountain scenery and the hospitality of its people. In 1990 a mere 8,000 tourists arrived in Afghanistan, bringing receipts of only about $1 million. Some potential attractions for the foreign visitor included Bamian, with its huge statues of the

Traffic conditions in Herat have improved with better paved roads. Today, Afghanistan's roads are filled with cars, motorcycles, buses, bicycles, and minivans.

Buddha, which were destroyed by the Taliban despite international protest. Work is under way to attempt to restore these statues. Thousands of painted caves, the Blue Mosque of Mazar-i-Sharif, the outstanding lakes of Bandi Amir, and the mountains of the Hindu Kush are also of interest. Some of the other major tourist attractions in Afghanistan include the Babur Gardens (recently restored by the Aga Khan Trust for Culture) and the British Cemetery (built in 1879 during the Second Anglo-Afghan War). With its stark natural beauty, and its many historical sites, Afghanistan has much potential for development in the tourist industry, but large areas of Afghanistan remain extremely dangerous and acts of violence occur regularly. Stability and security are of paramount importance to Afghanistan's recovery in this sector too.

## HYDROELECTRIC POWER

During the spring, melting snow from Afghanistan's mountains swells its numerous rivers and waterfalls to gushing torrents with huge potential for hydroelectric power. In the summer, when the flow is reduced to a mere trickle, dams and reservoirs are necessary to harness this power. There are six hydroelectric plants in Afghanistan, three in Kabul State and one each in Baghlan, Helmand, and Nangarhar. The largest is the Naghlu Dam Hydroelectric Power Plant, in Kabul.

# TRANSPORTATION

Afghanistan had 2,700 miles (4,345 km) of paved roads in 1979. The Kabul-Kandahar Highway was built in 1960 to connect these two largest cities and economic centers. It passed through five core provinces, skirting numerous isolated villages. More than two decades of war destroyed the highway, which had been mined, bombed, and neglected. Restoration of this main road was crucial to any development in the country. Approximately $190 million of USAID support to Afghanistan was spent on the Kabul-Kandahar Highway, which has not only been restored but also extended to form a "ring" road circling through Herat and Mazar-i-Sharif and back to Kabul. About 13.6 million people, approximately 66 percent of the population, live within 31 miles (50 km) of the Ring Road.

River navigation is another important method of transportation. There are about 750 miles (1,200 km) of navigable waterways in Afghanistan; the Amu Dar'ya is the most important. River ports on the Amu Dar'ya are also linked to Kabul by road.

In addition to four major domestic airports, Afghanistan has two international airports in Kabul and Kandahar. A third international airport is scheduled to be opened in Mazar-i-Sharif.

## INTERNET LINKS

**http://mail.gov.af/en**

This is the official website for Afghanistan's Ministry of Agriculture, Irrigation and Livestock (MAIL).

**www.bgs.ac.uk/AfghanMinerals/preciousStone.htm**

This is the official website of the Afghanistan Ministry of Mines, with information on geology, minerals, and mining.

**http://coin.fao.org/cms/media/8/13103724862880/faoaf_brochure_2011.pdf**

This brochure contains nformation on food production and agriculture in Afghanistan, including chapters on the agriculture production and productivity program as well as natural resource management.

# ENVIRONMENT

The magenta cliffs near Shahr-e-Zohak, or "Red City," between Kabul and Bamiya.

## 5

AFGHANISTAN HAS A VERY fragile ecosystem. The country's arable land and pastures are limited to the valleys and foothills, and the Hindu Kush has sparse vegetation except for the Sulaiman Range in the southwest. This arid terrain covers two-thirds of the country. Half of the rest of the land is desert.

## ENVIRONMENT IN CRISIS

Afghanistan's natural resource base and environment has deteriorated over the past three decades as a result of political instability, wars, and the excessive exploitation of natural resources, particularly wood. Since there was little industrial activity, industrialization's undesirable effects were few, but during the recent three decades of war, Afghanistan's ecosystem suffered rapid and irreversible damage. Widespread drought affects many parts of the country annually.

The decrease in agriculture led to the large-scale migration of Afghans from the rural areas to the cities. The resultant pressing need for urban expansion and development led to the clearing of forests and other precious vegetation. Rivers, irrigation canals, and wetlands dried up. Water tables were reduced. Water and soil pollution, salinization (a buildup of salt content in the soil), deforestation, and forced migration and resettlement, all resulted in the spread of environmental disease and increased desertification (when land degrades to barren and unproductive soil). Large tracts of forest and farmland were destroyed or burned to accommodate the bulging population.

Today, partly as a result of the past 30 years of political chaos, war, and conflict, Afghanistan's environment is in a critical condition. The National Environmental Protection Agency (NEPA) was created in 2005, and Afghanistan's first Environmental Law was passed in 2007. Soil degradation, deforestation, air and water pollution, overgrazing, and desertification are just some of the issues that need to be addressed.

## LEGACY OF WAR

Afghanistan is one of the most heavily mined countries in the world. The land mines are not only a legacy of the Taliban and Al-Qaeda fighting U.S. coalition forces. Many of the mines are left over from the Soviet occupations of Afghanistan from 1979 to 1989. Chemical weapons were also used during the war with the Soviet Union. The UN Office for the Coordination of Humanitarian Assistance (OCHA) to Afghanistan has estimated that there are still about 100,000 unexploded land mines in Afghanistan. Kabul is the most heavily mined capital city in the world, with approximately 74 percent of mined areas on grazing land, 19 percent on agricultural land, 5 percent in irrigation systems, and 1 percent on roads and in residential areas, respectively. Several international organizations, such as the UN Mine Action Center for Afghanistan, have been working to clear these mines for years.

Residents living on the hills of overcrowded cities like Kabul suffer from the high levels of pollution characteristic of urban areas in Afghanistan. The nation, still directing its resources to rebuilding, has to grapple with appalling sanitary conditions and perpetual traffic congestion brought about by its bulging population and poor infrastructure.

Unexploded cluster bombs, each one capable of destroying a large truck, are hazards that still threaten human life on a daily basis. Cluster bombs have a wide dispersal pattern and cannot be targeted precisely. They have a high initial failure rate. Numerous explosive "duds," which failed to detonate on initial impact, pose the same post-conflict problem as antipersonnel land mines. They are a serious and long-lasting threat to civilians, soldiers, and also to bomb clearance experts. It is estimated that mines contaminate approximately 301 square miles (780 square km) of land in Afghanistan. Currently this land is being cleared at a rate of about 13 square miles (35 square km) per year.

## DEFORESTATION

The most serious environmental problem facing Afghanistan is deforestation. Until a little over a decade ago, the ranges of Afghanistan were covered by dense cedar forest. Although many varieties of forests can be found here, only 1 to 2 percent of the land is forested today. There has been a 33 percent decrease from 1979. Environmental organizations recommend that 15 percent of the country should be forested in order to sustain air quality and prevent topsoil erosion.

The loss of natural resources and a four-year drought that emptied reservoirs and irrigation canals has compounded the damage to the country's infrastructure caused by fighting. The sharp fall in agricultural production has led to the further abuse of the natural resources of the environment. Extensive and uncontrolled logging has caused deforestation on an unprecedented scale. As the trees are cut down the rich topsoil is eroded by wind and rain and is no longer able to sustain growth. Environmental conservation has not been enforced and the exploitation of the country's meager forests continues unabated. Timber finds a ready market in neighboring countries, particularly Pakistan, and consequently truckloads of timber are smuggled over the border. Other truckloads of wood are brought into the cities to be used as fuel. Kabul has a population of more than 3 million people and many homes are without electricity. The only fuel available is wood, which is used both for cooking and for heating. Wood is also used in construction. The surrounding hillsides have been denuded of trees.

In the 1970s the Badghis and Takhar provinces of northern Afghanistan were covered with wild pistachio forests. These forests had provided thousands of families with a livelihood. Wild pistachio nuts used to be a major export of Afghanistan. Much of this forest, however, has disappeared in just three decades. The community forest warden project failed, fuelwood was stockpiled, and many trees were uprooted. The roots have been exported for use in herbal medicine, and the trees have been chopped up for fuel. Soil degradation due to rampant deforestation has intensified.

In 1999 crops and mulberry trees in the fertile region of Parwan near Kabul were burned by the Taliban military while the farmers were preparing for harvest. These farms were seen as natural obstacles to the pursuit of war. Vegetation all along the roads was removed for the same reason. In Nangarhar Province, in the east, most of the land along the Kabul—Turkham Highway was turned into wasteland.

The large-scale deforestation has led to severe erosion of fertile soils. The topography of the terrain accelerates such erosion. Deforestation has resulted in widespread flooding and in landslides in the Salang Valley, resulting in the loss of many lives. The washing away of topsoil and humus has created ever more arid conditions, and stunted the growth of crops.

Afghanistan is located in a tectonically active region and is prone to strong, damaging earthquakes. Erosion has resulted in avalanches in the Salang Valley.

## WILDLIFE

Afghanistan's wildlife heritage is under threat as habitat for animals and plants is disappearing. The Hindu Kush and Pamir mountains are home to a type of goat called a markhor (*Capra falconeri*) that lives only in Afghanistan and neighboring territories, and is considered globally threatened. The area is also home to rare mountain leopards, gazelles, Marco Polo sheep, urial sheep, Asiatic bears, and snow leopards. The Caspian tiger is considered extinct, and fewer than 100 snow leopards survive. Their pelts fetch a very high price on the black markets of the world, making them highly susceptible to being poached. The skins of other such internationally protected or endangered animals as leopards, tigers, foxes, and jackals can be bought all over the country. Marco Polo sheep and ibex are hunted for food.

Dynamite fishing has become common and threatens not only the survival of the numerous species of fish in the mountain streams there but also other animals in the vicinity.

The prospects for the wildlife of the Wakhan Corridor are more encouraging because the area escaped much of the recent conflict and is free of land mines. The area is grazed by the yurt-dwelling Kyrgyz and Wakhi herders who have responded well to recent requests to hand in arms and stop hunting. Furthermore the area borders Tajikstan, Pakistan, and China so the region's snow leopards, Marco Polo sheep, brown bear, wolves, and Asian ibex are able to migrate and find refuge.

## POLLUTION

The pollutants from industrial parks of countries of the Aral sedimentary basin, such as Iran, Turkmenistan, and Uzbekistan, contribute to the poor quality of air in cities. Cross-boundary pollution is a threat to Afghanistan's environment as there are too few industries in Afghanistan, yet, to cause much pollution. Nonetheless the use of heavy war machinery and weapons for so long has polluted or contaminated the soil in most areas of the country.

With most of the country's infrastructure destroyed, basic sanitation is almost nonexistent. Open sewers are the norm. The water is often contaminated by sewage and contains harmful bacteria such as *E. coli.*

The poverty and displacement caused by war drove many people from the countryside to the cities. Combined with the return of refugees, the populations of the cities have swelled, and the heavy demand this has placed on the very weak infrastructure has made the situation very critical, even hazardous, to the environment. The air and water quality in most cities has deteriorated sharply due to the use of wood as fuel, unregulated vehicle traffic, and industrial development.

Solid waste disposal is a major problem. Today there are still no proper landfills in many cities and none of the dumpsites are designed to prevent groundwater contamination or toxic air pollution from burning waste. Most dumps are sited upstream from cities. As a result their contents and seepage are washed down by the rain, contaminating water supplies and worsening the already dire sanitation problems in the cities.

International organizations such as the UN are urging the country to initiate efforts to reconstruct or restore the environment. It is hoped that with a stable government in place it will be possible to work toward preserving and sustaining the environment. If measures to halt further damage are delayed, there may be no turning back.

Smoke from the wood fires used for heating and cooking covers the interiors of homes with soot. In the evenings and early mornings the Kabul sky is blanketed with smoke from these fires.

## INTERNET LINKS

**www.un.org/cyberschoolbus/banmines/schools/afgbackground.asp**

This official UN website contains information about the land mine issue in Afghanistan and links to further information on the country.

**www.unep.org/pdf/UNEP_in_Afghanistan.pdf**

This is the official website of the UN Environment Program, with a link to a pdf document on laying the foundations for sustainable development in Afghanistan.

**www.afghan-web.com/environment/deforestation.html**

This website contains a link to information about the causes of deforestation in Afghanistan.

# AFGHANS

A family in Kabul. As Afghans hail from various ethnic groups and because of the fragility and intricacy of Afghanistan's multicultural and multiethnic social fabric, tribe affiliations have become integral to the average Afghan's identity.

# 6

RELIABLE POPULATION STATISTICS for Afghanistan have always been difficult to obtain because of the instability in the country. To escape the Soviet occupation, millions of Afghans fled from their homes to safety in refugee camps in the neighboring countries of Pakistan and Iran.

As civil war between various factions continued following the Soviet withdrawal, the number of civilians fleeing the country increased. Afghanistan became the center of the world's worst refugee crisis. By 1990 there were 6.3 million civilians in exile—3.3 million in Pakistan and 3 million in Iran. More than 300 villages were established in Pakistan for the mainly ethnic Pashtun refugees. In Iran mostly ethnic Tajiks, Uzbeks, and Hazaras lived and found work in local communities.

The movement of civilians reflected the location of fighting in the country, with many refugees returning to peaceful parts of the country. As the countryside had been ravaged, making a living from agriculture became unviable. Refugees flooded into the cities to look for work. Afghanistan has a population growth rate of about 2.3 percent in rural areas and 4.7 percent in urban areas, reflecting the migration to urban centers. In 2005 the population was about 25 million people. This is an unfortunate increase for a country in the midst of economic recovery, national reconstruction, and transformation after more than three decades of turmoil and war—a war that took the lives of more than a million people—and five years of extreme repression under the Taliban.

The first official population census in Afghanistan was conducted in 1979 when the population registered at just over 15 million and included more than 2.5 million nomads. The census was not completed because of the Soviet invasion, so there has always been uncertainty over the accuracy of this figure. In 2012 the population of Afghanistan was estimated to be about 31 million. The largest single ethnic group is the Pashtun, at 42 percent of the population.

A Pashtun man in Afghanistan. Many Afghan men wear turbans tied in a way that signifies affiliation with an ethnic group.

Afghans are a potpourri of ethnic and linguistic groups. This is the result of the intermingling of various races that entered Afghanistan who eventually intermarried and blended with the local population, leaving their imprint on both the social makeup and cultural development of the country.

Most of the population, such as the Pashtun, Tajik, Nuristani, and Baluchi, belong to the Mediterranean subgroup of the Caucasoid race, to which most of the people of the Mediterranean and Middle Eastern countries also belong.

Besides the Caucasoid, there are two other main physical types in Afghanistan—the Mongoloid and the Australoid. The Hazara, Turkmen (also known as Turkoman), Uzbek, Kyrgyz, and Aimaq are Mongoloid, and the Brahui are Australoid.

## PASHTUNS

Slightly less than half the country's population is Pashtun. They have traditionally been the most powerful of all the groups in Afghanistan. They regard themselves as the true Afghans. In India and Pakistan they are known as Pathans. As a group they are still synonymous with strength and fortitude. The Pashtuns are currently and historically the dominant political group in Afghanistan. Pashtuns appear to have lived in Afghanistan since the beginning of recorded history. Although their origin is obscure, they are believed to be of Aryan stock. Their language, Pushtu, belongs to the Indo-European group of languages and is related to the Persian Farsi. Pushtu is written in the Perso-Arabic script.

In one version of the legend, Qais, who is said to have been descended from King Saul and from one of the lost peoples of Israel, is believed to be the person to whom the Pashtuns owe their ancestry. Qais, according to the Pashtuns, was chosen by the Muslim Prophet Muhammad to spread Islam in Afghanistan. In another version, Afghana, a grandson of King Saul of the tribe of Benjamin, is thought to have led his 40 sons to the hills of Ghor in the western part of Hazarajat, making him the ancestor of the Afghans.

The Pashtuns live in an area extending from the Pamir Mountains, north of Afghanistan, across the Sulaiman Range and the Helmand Valley all the way to Herat and the Iranian border. They began venturing out of this mountainous vastness only in the 11th century, when they joined the armies of Mahmud of Ghazni in his conquest of India. Warfare has since then become an integral part of a Pashtun's life; even today the Pashtuns habitually carry firearms.

There are about 60 Pashtun tribes but the two main Pashtun groups are the Ghilzais and the Durranis, who are also known as Abdalis. The Ghilzais are also known as Khiljis or Ghaljis and are the single most populous Pashtun tribe in Afghanistan. They occupy the north of Kandahar, extending east toward the Sulaiman Mountains. The Ghilzais are concentrated in an area spanning Ghazni and Kalat-i-Ghilzai eastward into western Pakistan, but are predominantly a nomadic group, unlike the Durrani who can be found in permanent settlements. The Ghilzais came to prominence in the 17th century when the Abdalis were banished by the Shah of Persia.

A Tajik family sits outside their home in Kabul.

The Ghilzais seized control of Kandahar, invaded and conquered Persia, and ruled there for a short period. In 1747 when the Durrani ruler Ahmad Shah came into power, the Ghilzais were forced to accept his rule. The Ghilzais have always played a crucial role in the commercial and military sectors of Afghanistan.

Physically the Pashtuns resemble true Aryan stock. They are typically tall and fair, often with aquiline features and black or brown hair and brown eyes, although hazel or even blue eyes are not uncommon.

## TAJIKS

The Tajiks are of Iranian origin and, like the Pashtuns, can be divided into two principal groups. One group of Tajiks, who are Shi'a Muslims, lives mainly in the mountainous regions of Badakhshan and the Wakhan Valley. They are farmers who live in villages that are often extremely poverty stricken.

The other group of Tajiks lives on the plains mainly in the provinces of Herat and Paarwan and around major towns such as Kabul, Bamian, and Herat. They are urban dwellers and form a large part of the middle class in the larger towns. These Tajiks are Sunni Muslims and are skilled artisans and traders. Many are also farmers, and the zamindars, or landowners, among

The Pashtuns are renowned throughout the world for their prowess on the battlefield. The most successful wars against the British in the 19th century were conducted by the Pashtuns.

them are accepted as village leaders. Although tribal organizations no longer exist for this group, a strong communal feeling lives on among them.

The Tajiks are of Mediterranean stock and are generally tall with light skin and black hair, although red or even blond hair is sometimes seen. In the north the Tajiks have more Mongoloid features.

## NURISTANIS

Other Muslims often referred to Nuristanis as Kafirs, or unbelievers in Islam, in the past. They were called this because they had belonged to an independent group until Amir Abdur Rahman Khan conquered them in 1896 and converted them to Islam.

Nuristanis speak a unique Indo-European language and live mainly in the East of the country. Nuristan is located on the southern slopes of the Hindu Kush, and is spread over an area of four valleys, with each valley having its own distinct dialect: Kati, Waigali, Ashkun, and Parsun.

Physically most Nuristanis resemble Mediterranean stock. They are slight of build, with light brown skin, slender noses, above-average height, and black to sometimes blond hair.

Nuristanis are very conservative, place great emphasis on family ties, and are known and respected for their great physical endurance. Nuristani men traditionally wear goatskin coats over a cotton shirt; short, full cotton trousers; leggings; and soft leather boots.

## HAZARAS

The Hazaras live among the mountains and valleys of central Afghanistan. Hazarajat (or Hazarestan) is a bare, dry region, watered by canals carefully constructed to carry as much water as possible from the few springs that are to be found. Crop cultivation is limited because of the poor soil and lack of water. Traditionally most of the Hazaras are shepherds who follow seasonal grazing grounds. They are hardworking and frugal, but because of the adverse conditions in the region, they have been unable to prosper. Many of them have chosen to join the army, and others have been forced to seek menial labor in the cities.

Hazaras are of Mongoloid stock and are traditionally believed to be descended from the soldiers of Genghis Khan's army that swept through Afghanistan in the 13th century. Unlike the majority of Afghanistan's population, who are Sunni, most Hazaras are Shi'a Muslims. Some Hazaras are followers of the Ismaili sect while a small number of them are Sunni Muslims.

Hazara men wear skullcaps and are clean-shaven. The women wear long dresses instead of the baggy trousers that are commonly worn elsewhere in Afghanistan.

Kirghiz women at their yurt camp in Little Pamir, Wakhan. They wear bright red dresses, white flowing headdresses, and elaborate necklaces made of coins, silver pieces, and beads.

## UZBEKS AND OTHER TURKISH MINORITIES

North of the Hindu Kush area are inhabitants descended from Central Asian Turks, or Tartars. The largest group is the Uzbeks. They are mostly farmers and breed animals, including horses and Karakul sheep. Additionally, they produce crafts and animal by-products, which bring supplementary income to their communities. A very important part of their economy is the production of carpets. Uzbeks have Turkish features and are usually fairer than other Afghans.

The Turkmen number about 400,000 and live along the southern bank of the Amu Dar'ya. They arrived in the 1920s and 1930s along with many thousands of Uzbeks as refugees to escape repression by the Soviet Union after their participation in the unsuccessful Basmachi Revolt. The Kyrgyz, who number about 35,000, made their homes in the narrow Wakhan Corridor. Both groups are nomads of Mongoloid descent.

Another Turkish group, the Qizilbash, or redheads, so named because they wore red skullcaps, were taken into Afghanistan by the Persian ruler Nadir Shah Afshar in the 18th century to garrison Kabul. Today their descendants, who are Imami Shi'a, occupy a separate quarter of Kabul and Kandahar and are employed in the government civil service and as craftspeople and clerks. Many are also traders. To the north of Afghanistan are several nomadic groups, such as the Kazakhs, Karlug, and Chagatai Turks. These people speak an archaic form of Turkish and often also speak Farsi. The men wear large, soft leather boots, belted cloaks, and turbans. Clothing typical of the area is the greatcoat with sleeves large enough to envelop the hands and to keep them warm during cold weather.

*Except for some of the Pashtun areas in the south and the east of the country, few Afghans are of a single ethnic descent. Over the centuries there has been much intermarriage among the different groups in contact with each other in the same regions. In the north, among the Tajiks and the Uzbeks, a surprising mixture of Caucasoid and Mongoloid features is often found. Red or blond hair and blue eyes are sometimes seen with the epicanthic fold and high cheekbones. Similarly blue- or green-eyed Baluchis and Brahui, who are normally dark-skinned, are not uncommon.*

## NOMADS

Because much of Afghanistan's land is barren and arid, it is not surprising that a portion of the country's population is nomadic or semi-nomadic. The nomads roam the land, moving with the seasons, looking for grazing sites for their herds.

They are fiercely conservative and abhor change. To survive the harsh environment, nomads need to be extremely hardy and tenacious, both physically and mentally. They are proud of their way of life and disdain people who live in cities. The worst thing a nomadic mother can say to a disobedient daughter is, "May you marry a town dweller!"

The Kharoti Powindahs Ghilzais, also known as Kuchis, are the best known of the nomads. The Kharoti clan is the second-largest Ghilzai Pashtun tribal group. They used to migrate annually across the border into Pakistan in the tens of thousands to trade, their camels and donkeys laden with everything they owned or needed, from their tents to their babies.

Once across the border they sold their wares, such as wool and hides. On their return trip they brought back goods either for their own use or for selling in Afghanistan. The Kharoti Powindahs traveled at night and camped during the day. The Kuchi now are nomadic herdsmen and their four main animals are sheep, goats, camels, and donkeys. They have a high illiteracy rate because the children usually do not attend school. Children as young as 9 years old are shepherds. There are estimated to be about 3 million Kuchi in Afghanistan with at least 60 percent remaining fully nomadic and more than 100,000 displaced in southern Afghanistan due to drought.

Kharoti Powindah men are tall, with piercing eyes, and full mustaches. They wear large turbans and are invariably armed with a dagger and rifle each.

The women wear colorful long-sleeved dresses over trousers and cover their heads with long shawls. They also often don heavy silver bracelets on their wrists and ankles and display other ornaments. These accessories make them look very similar to the Gypsies who roam the length and breadth of Europe and Asia. Perhaps the women's bright clothes and ornaments compensate for the dull, colorless landscape in which they live. The extreme and discriminatory rule of the former Taliban government, however, decreed that a woman be covered with the burka while outside her home.

## OTHERS

There are many groups of Afghans who call themselves Sayyid and claim Arab descent. They speak a form of Arabic.

Thousands of Hindus and Sikhs from the Indian subcontinent have also settled in Afghanistan and can be found mainly in the towns. Most have become Afghan citizens.

## INTERNET LINKS

**www.gl.iit.edu/govdocs/afghanistan/EthnicityAndTribe.html**

This webpage contains information about Afghanistan's religious sects and ethnic, linguistic, and tribal groups.

**www.afghan-bios.info/database.html**

This database has extensive links to who is who in Afghanistan, including tribal and individual profiles.

**www.minorityrights.org/5429/afghanistan/afghanistan-overview.html**

The World Directory of Minorities and Indigenous Peoples provides information on Afghanistan and links to information on the ethnic groups within the country.

The Brahui, who are found in the southwest, are made up of a confederation of 29 tribes. They are distinguished from their Baluchi and Pashtun neighbors by language. The Pashtun and Baluchi speak Indo-Iranian languages. The Brahui speak a Dravidian language. They are primarily nomadic shepherds.

# LIFESTYLE

Locals from Garozarak, a remote village in the Ghor province of Afghanistan, use mules to move large bundles of densely packed grass, known as *khuzba*, for cooking and heating.

## 7

THE UNWRITTEN LAWS AND CODES of conduct of *Pashtunwali* (PUHSH-toon-WAH-lee) reign supreme in Afghanistan. Although basically belonging to the Pashtuns, *Pashtunwali* is recognized and upheld by all Afghans.

Self-pride and tribe and family honor take precedence over everything else. Life is taken or sacrificed at the slightest hint of insult or loss of honor. Injustices to self or family or even tribe are not easily forgotten or forgiven. Thus feuds can sometimes go on for generations.

Afghan society is patriarchal. The son takes his bride to the ancestral home, where often several generations live together in one home or nearby in the same village. Even when Afghans migrate to towns and cities or move to other villages, family members still get together for important events, and an avid interest is taken in everyone else's affairs.

Every family is headed by a patriarch, and families belonging to a particular ethnic group are, in turn, led by a khan. All important judgments and decisions are made by the local council, or *jirga* (jorhr-GAH). Everyone has a right to voice an opinion, but the final decision is made by the *jirga* and must be adhered to without exception.

Apart from the decision making and the passing of judgment, the khan is also responsible for the safety and prosperity of his village. He must be a person with moral strength, wisdom, piety, bravery, and remarkable hospitality. He must also be of impeccable ancestry.

The *Pashtunwali* (PUHSH-toon-WAH-lee) covers a large area of human behavior, the most important being honor, vengeance, and hospitality. Every child is indoctrinated into its principles from birth. Any breach can be severely punishable, with anything from ostracism and exile to death.

Afghanistan is a rural kingdom with about 80 percent of the population engaged in agriculture. The remaining 20 percent are nomads who travel long distances between their *yaylaqs* (summer quarters) in the highlands and their *qishlaqs* (winter quarters) in the lowlands. People who own between 50 and 500 acres (20.23 and 202.3 ha) of land are called the landed gentry and they may often be involved in commerce and government.

To the Afghan nothing is as despicable as cowardice. Personal or family honor, *ghairat* (gheh-RAHT), must be upheld at all costs. Promises made, no matter what the circumstances, must always be kept.

Fierce family and ethnic group or tribe affiliation leads to the Afghan belief in the right to raid other groups to obtain food and provisions for their own. This is a harsh country, and the availability of water is vital; groups have to compete for what little is available. Life is devoid of all but the most basic material necessities, so a sense of pride and belonging is what makes life worth living. The Afghan is a fighter, battling against the hard conditions of his or her lot in life.

Much of this way of life is left behind when the villager moves to the towns and cities. Society there is no longer classless; the educated and the rich form the upper crust of society. The professionals, teachers, and government and industrial employees make up the bulk of a growing middle class. Back home in the villages the elders are revered, and their advice is sought and always heeded. In urban Afghanistan such values no longer hold, and the elderly often feel unwanted and lost.

## LIFE IN THE VILLAGES

The villages in Afghanistan are clustered around the larger towns and cities. The flat-roofed houses are built with bricks and plastered with a mixture of mud and straw. In the west, along the border with Iran, and in the northern plains, are found square, domed roofs. In the south the nomads and semi-nomads build semicircular, beehive-shaped reed huts.

Most houses have enclosed compounds that shelter livestock and boast sheds for storage. In each of these houses, the cooking area and the general living space where the family works and plays also share that compound.

Women walk to the nearest stream or pool to collect water, bathe, and do the laundry. Some of the more affluent households have their own artificially made pools or streams, called *jooyi* (joo-YEE). The trips to the streams provide the women with a chance to get away from home for a while and to socialize with each other.

Accommodation in the villages is always provided for travelers. Where circumstances permit, carpeted rooms are kept to entertain guests in the

## THE CODES OF *PASHTUNWALI*

*Louis Dupree, in his book* Afghanistan, *summarizes the rules of* Pashtunwali *as follows:*

- *To avenge blood.*
- *To fight to the death for a person who has taken refuge with me no matter what his lineage.*
- *To defend to the last any property entrusted to me.*
- *To be hospitable and provide for the safety of the person and property of guests.*
- *To refrain from killing a woman, a Hindu, a minstrel, or a boy not yet circumcised.*
- *To pardon an offence on the intercession of a woman of the offender's lineage, a Sayyid or a mullah. [An exception is made in the case of murder: only blood or blood money can erase this crime.]*
- *To punish all adulterers with death.*
- *To refrain from killing a man who has entered a mosque or the shrine of a holy man so long as he remains within its precincts, also to spare a man in battle who begs for quarter.*

home. Mosques double up as schools and often also provide meeting places for the local *jirga*. In some villages communal affairs are conducted under shady trees.

Household furnishings are simple, consisting of cooking utensils, basic dishes, and some heirlooms, such as religious mementos, weapons, brass or copper utensils, and storage chests and containers. Large earthenware pots are used to store grains. Some villagers possess string beds, but most sleep on mattresses that are laid out on the floor at night and neatly stacked in a corner during the day.

The flat roofs are used in summer for sleeping and for drying fruits and vegetables. An earthen platform is often built in front of the house for the same purpose. In summer food is cooked outdoors. Charcoal and dung patties, together with roots and branches, are burned for fuel. The patties are made by the women and children, who collect the manure, form it into patties, and slap them onto walls and rocks to dry.

Mud and brick structures that look like block houses, with rectangular holes for air circulation, are built to dry grapes in order to make raisins. Windmills are found in Herat, but they pump water only during the "time of the 120 days' wind," which falls between June and September.

The Afghans have invented a simple but ingenious system of keeping themselves warm. In the villages south of the Hindu Kush, houses have hot-air tunnels, or *tawkhanah*, built under the floor and a fire at one end warms up the whole floor. In other places, a small, low table is placed over a charcoal brazier, and a blanket is spread over this table to contain the heat. The family sits around the table to keep warm. This unique system is called *sandali*.

## NOMADIC LIFE

The nomads follow their herds to summer and winter grazing grounds. The semi-nomads move in summer to pastures with their herds and return in winter to tend crops on their farms. The nomads provide several services to the villagers. Besides supplying animal products, they form lines of communication between different regions. The animal dung left when they pass over the fields helps to fertilize the land. Often the nomads act as moneylenders, lending money to the farmers.

The tents of the nomads are built with or without frames. Frameless tents are built with black goats' hair and come in three major styles: the south and western Durrani Pashtun tent; the eastern and northern Ghilzai tent; and the barrel-vaulted tent found in Baluchistan. A fourth style of frameless tent, *arabi*, is found among the Aimaq. The semi-nomads live in yurts, tents with a portable lattice-like framework. The frame is covered with reeds and a number of woven colored bands. The pole at the top of the wood-framed foundation is supported by a series of long poles tied with special knots. The poles are curved to fit into a slotted, hollow wooden disk at the top of the yurt (yerht). Felt, often elaborately decorated, is tied onto the frame, with the design on the inside. The door is made of carved wood.

Nomadic migration resembles a military operation. The younger shepherds move along the higher trails with the sheep and goats, while the older people and children move along lower valley trails with the other animals. They may travel 3 to 15 miles (5 to 24 km) a day, and when they stop for the night, the men settle the animals down and stand guard. The rest of the work is done by the women; they put up and dismantle the tents, load and unload the pack animals, do the housework, and prepare the food. Today much of the land, roamed by these nomads for centuries, is riddled with land mines and cluster bombs.

## URBAN AFGHANISTAN

Towns in Afghanistan are usually situated at the intersections of major trails or near the larger rivers. Since 1953 asphalt roads have been built in most towns, but many of these roads have since been destroyed during the decades of war and conflict. Towns act as commercial, administrative, and communication centers for the surrounding villages.

Agricultural produce, handicrafts, and raw materials are taken to towns by villagers to be sent on to cities. Transportation within towns is usually by horse cart. Civil servants, who are involved in the administration of the surrounding villages, and landlords, who own land in the villages, generally prefer to live in the towns.

Finished goods from cities are shipped by truck to towns. There they are sold in the bazaar (marketplace) or the main street of the town; most shop owners live in rooms above their shops. Aside from these goods, various kinds of artisans providing services needed by the villagers can also be found in the bazaars.

*Caravanserais* (kaa-ra-waan-sa-rais), or traditional inns, and *chaikhanas* (chaa-ee-kha-nahs), or the popular teahouses, are found in the towns. The *caravanserais* were especially built to shelter men, animals, and goods along ancient caravan routes. In the *chaikhanas* men gather to smoke water pipes, drink strongly brewed tea, and exchange the latest news. The Muslim prohibition against alcohol is almost universally observed.

Summer yurts in a semi-nomad Aimaq camp between Chakhcharan and Jam in Pal-Kotal-i-Guk. The nomads favor tents that can easily be put up or dismantled. The tents are woven from goats' hair, which is considerably more durable than sheep's wool.

A mobile phone store in Herat. City life in Afghanistan today features many modern facilities.

Unlike in the past, when news was spread solely by word of mouth, there are radios in most of the *chaikhanas* nowadays. News is heard and discussed, and patrons listen to music and songs from Indian movies. Afghanistan has no homegrown movie industry. Indian movies are very popular throughout the country, and there are theaters in some of the major towns and cities.

Since antiquity cities have sprung up where major routes meet and provide access to the outside world. The five main cities of Afghanistan are Kabul, Kandahar, Herat, Mazar-i-Sharif, all with populations of more than 100,000, and Kunduz. Kabul is by far the largest city in Afghanistan. Between 1999 and 2002 the city's population grew at 15 percent a year and was estimated at 3 million in 2004. This represents a yearly increase of about 150,000 people, or 20,000 households, all needing land and access to services. In 2009 the population of Kabul was estimated at 3.573 million. It is estimated that 80 percent of the population still lives in informal settlements, which cover over half of the residential area. These informal settlements lack all basic infrastructure. Just as in the towns, there are bazaars in the cities on appropriately larger scales. The historic Murad Khane bazaar of Kabul was one of the busiest markets in Central Asia. Almost every kind of merchandise imaginable was sold in its own special section there. Goods produced both on a small scale by individuals and in much greater volume by factories were either sold locally in the bazaars or exported. However, by 2008, after having been on the front line of the war, Murad Khane was an impoverished slum and earmarked for demolition.

Many Hazaras have moved to Kabul. Some became self-employed, trading in wood products, butter, and lard, or making aluminum pots and pans. Most, however, work as laborers, gathering at specific spots every morning for foremen to recruit them. Many Tajiks move to cities to work as drivers. Their hard-earned savings are then mostly used to buy their own land or trucks.

# CHANGING LIFESTYLE

After decades of turmoil, the traditional life of both urban and rural societies has disintegrated. At least two generations of children have lost their childhoods. Their minds and bodies are scarred by the death and destruction they have witnessed around them. Dignity and self-reliance were destroyed by living in refugee camps.

With as many as 10,000 villages ravaged and flattened, a large percentage of the rural population has moved to the cities. These people, along with the millions of returning refugees, have swelled urban populations.

The government, with aid from such international institutions as the World Bank, has initiated a program of restoration of infrastructures and other public utilities. Clinics, hospitals, commercial institutions, and schools are being built and restored. Fewer than a million children in Afghanistan went to school during the Taliban's reign. Now there are more than 6 million children registered in schools and about one-third of them are girls. Since 2011 UNICEF and its partners—including the World Health Organization (WHO) and the government of Afghanistan—have ensured that 10 million Afghan children have been vaccinated against the polio virus. This is an ongoing process with the aim of eradicating polio from Afghanistan.

The Turquoise Mountain Foundation, supported by President Karzai and Britain's Prince Charles, was established with the aim of restoring Murad Khane, reviving Afghanistan's craft industry, and setting up the Institute for Afghan Arts and Architecture. Shops were reconstructed, trenches were dug for electricity and sanitation, and the alleyways were cleared of trash. Historically significant buildings, such as Babur Gardens, were restored and a primary school was set up to provide education to local children.

The Aga Khan Foundation is a part of the Aga Khan Development Network (AKDN). The Foundation focuses on a small number of specific development problems by forming intellectual and financial partnerships with organizations sharing its objectives. Most Foundation grants are made to grassroots organizations testing innovative approaches in the field. With a small staff, a host of cooperating agencies, and thousands of volunteers, the Foundation reaches out to vulnerable populations on four continents, irrespective of their race, religion, political persuasion, or gender. One of their agencies, the Aga Khan Trust for Culture (AKTC), is involved in physical, social, cultural, and economic revitalization of communities in the Muslim world. They are committed to the preservation of historic buildings in Afghanistan and elsewhere. They have been working to prove that cultural heritage can become a catalyst for positive change.

## ROLE OF WOMEN

Women in Afghanistan have traditionally occupied secondary roles in society. They must obey their fathers or husbands and seek their permission for almost everything they do. Nevertheless women are far from being weak; they wield much power and influence in decision making in their own homes, where they reign supreme as homemakers.

The women of rural Afghanistan are physically strong and work just as hard as the men. They are reputed to be courageous, resilient, and well able to face the dangers of their environment. Most of them have learned to handle firearms and to use them for protection against robbers and wild animals.

In marriage and divorce, Afghanistan follows Islamic laws. A man only needs to repeat "I divorce you" three times in front of a witness to divorce his wife. A woman, on the other hand, has to appear before a judge with reasons for a divorce. Simple though it may sound, divorce is not common. A great deal of social stigma is attached to divorce. Moreover the requirement to pay alimony—as well as the difficulty in replacing a wife, who plays an important role in the management of the home, the land, and livestock—makes divorce unattractive to most men. Polygamy is permitted in Islam, and a man is allowed to take up to four wives, a practice that is not very common in Afghanistan. Adultery is punishable by death for both men and women, according to Islamic laws.

Property is usually divided among the sons, the daughters having received their share as dowry. Widows are provided for—a widow receives one-eighth of her husband's property and the assurance of a home and protection by his family. She also controls the jewelry, passing it on to her daughters or daughters-in-law as she likes.

# NATIONAL GEOGRAPHIC—FACE OF AN AFGHAN GIRL

*In 1985 the face of an Afghan girl was featured on the cover of* National Geographic *magazine. Seventeen years after the photograph was taken, the Pashtun girl, now a symbol of the tragic plight of Afghan women and refugees from the war-torn country, was tracked down by the magazine. Her name is Sharbat Gula. The young woman, worn down by years of hardship and toil, now lives in a remote part of Afghanistan with her husband and children. The intense and piercing glare in her captivating green eyes still speaks of the tragedy of a country wracked by a quarter century of war.*

Women in rural Afghanistan enjoy greater freedom than their sisters in the towns in dressing. They do not have to wear the *chadari* (chawdari), or burka, a voluminous outer garment with only a slit or net for the eyes. The need for them to work side by side with their men in the fields frees them from wearing such cumbersome clothing. However, they must keep their distance from men other than their family members. The women of the nomadic groups move freely, going about their daily affairs unrestricted by rules of gender segregation.

Amanullah Khan, in the 1920s, tried to emancipate women by encouraging coeducation, removing the veil requirement, and promoting the use of Western dress. This angered the religious and conservative elements of Afghan society and contributed to his eventual downfall. During the 1960s and 1970s, under the progressive constitution of Zahir Shah, and during the years of Soviet occupation, many women in the larger cities, especially Kabul, where European influence is most strongly felt, took to wearing Western dress. The communist government's vigorous effort to improve the status of women constituted one of the reasons for widespread rebellion by conservative Afghans.

Women were denied any freedom or basic human rights by the fundamentalist mujahideen warlords who ruled Afghanistan during the civil war between 1992 and 1996. The Taliban regime continued the intolerance and brutality toward women. Purdah and the wearing of the *chadari* had not been enforced in the past. The Taliban, however, made it absolutely compulsory, and women were beaten if they violated any of the rules imposed

An outspoken and fierce champion of women's rights in Afghanistan—Fawzia Koofi. She was first elected to parliament in 2005 and won a seat again in 2010. She has also declared her intention to run for the presidency in the 2014 elections.

on them. A woman was not allowed to leave home without being escorted by a male blood relative. Girls were forbidden to attend school and women were not allowed to work. Young girls were forced into marriage and thousands of women were physically assaulted. Now, with the collapse of the Taliban regime, the women in Afghanistan are liberated from the restrictions that were imposed upon them. Modern dressing has developed; under the new constitution women are on equal footing with men. They are guaranteed 25 percent of the seats in the *Wolesi Jirga* and 30 percent in the provincial councils. Sixty-nine women have been appointed as new lawmakers after the parliamentary elections of September 2010. An Afghan women's rights activist, Malalai Joya, has also been named a new parliamentarian in the *Wolesi Jirga*.

Many Afghan women have returned to work. There are many female professionals. Nongovernmental organizations, or NGOs, and other groups are conducting classes and lessons for women in crafts such as tailoring. The war has left many Afghan widows to fend for themselves and their children. Others are burdened with looking after men who were maimed or crippled. Postwar Afghanistan seems ready to improve the social position of women and to give women a bigger role in the establishment of democracy in the state.

Aid Afghanistan for Education (AAE) is dedicated to empowering women and reviving the education system in Afghanistan. In 1996 the organization was founded by Hassina Sherjan, who had left Afghanistan as a refugee in 1979. She returned to Afghanistan in 1999 and established five clandestine classes for girls. Through these classes 250 girls were educated and able to integrate back into the school system after the defeat of the Taliban. Since then AAE has established many other schools, not just in Kabul, but also in Ghazni, Wardak, Parwan, and Bamyan provinces. AAE considers the education of Afghan children to be critical in the move toward a more stable, peaceful, and prosperous future.

In 2012 Afghanistan opened its first female-only Internet café. Although the Taliban were toppled over a decade ago women may still be harassed by their countrymen. The modest café was named after Sahar Gul, a 15-year-old Afghan girl who was brutally tortured by her husband and in-laws after refusing to obey her husband's request to work as a prostitute. The Afghan activist group YoungWomen4Change set up the Internet café to give women a chance to connect with the world in a totally secure environment. A British charity donated the computers. Fundraising both in Afghanistan and abroad secured the $1,000 a month needed to run the café, although it is hoped that it will be self-sustaining in the future. Nevertheless, much still needs to be done to ensure that all Afghan women are treated with respect, granted basic human rights, given equal career opportunities. In addition it should be ensured that girls are granted a proper education, especially in provinces that still practice strict and sometimes brutal mujahideen- and Taliban-influenced gender discrimination.

## FAMILY RELATIONSHIPS

Families in Afghanistan are close-knit, and a strong sense of responsibility exists toward all members of the nuclear as well as the extended family. The extended family often includes all those who can trace descent from a common ancestor. Similarly kinship includes those whose ancestors were brothers.

As is the norm in most Islamic societies, there are no family names, and recognition is given by reference to the fathers. In spite of this, the original family of most Afghans is known by all. Any disgrace suffered or honor earned by an individual is felt by all those who claim kinship. Blood relationships are also given due distinction. Paternal uncles are called *kaka* (kaw-kaw) and maternal uncles are called *mama* (maw-maw). Every kinship tie is well defined and recognized.

Another important aspect of Afghan family relationships is the order of birth. Upon the death of the father, the eldest son, by virtue of his birth rank, assumes authority and becomes the most powerful in the family and receives a larger share of the inheritance.

In urban areas, where Western culture has greater influence, the family unit often consists of the nuclear family alone. When a son marries, he stays with his parents only a short while before moving out to his own home with

In the past, if a girl died after the engagement, her family would replace her with another girl from the family. If the husband died after marriage, a brother of the husband would take the widow as his wife. This custom is no longer popular.

his bride. The decision to move often depends on the financial position or capacity of the family.

## MARRIAGE

In many Afghan stories and folklore, marriage is based on romance. In reality, however, most marriages in Afghanistan are arranged by parents and relatives. There is a strict moral code, and chastity is prescribed for unmarried men and women.

Marriages are often arranged when the couple are still children. However, a man does not marry until he is about 18 to 20 years of age. According to the constitution, a girl must be at least 16 years old and must agree to the arranged marriage. Marriages between cousins, especially paternal ones, are greatly favored as they are seen to increase or perpetuate the already strong family ties. In a forced marriage, one of the partners is not willing to participate and various degrees of coercion are involved. In an arranged marriage the families make all the decisions but individuals getting married can choose whether to get married or not. In many cases the distinction between a forced or arranged marriage is blurred. In some of the worst cases, girls as young as eight years old have been forced into marriage. These forced and early marriages deprive the girls of an education and their basic human rights, but forced marriage is a cultural practice in Afghanistan. Marriages are sometimes used to settle debts or to strengthen family status through social alliances.

In marriages within a family, the bride price, which can often be steep, is forfeited. Otherwise bride price is paid by the groom's family to compensate for the loss of a valuable family member. A dowry is paid by the family of the bride, and this consists of household goods, which in the urban society include electrical appliances and other modern gadgets.

When the parents decide that their children are ready for marriage, a relative is usually sought to act as a go-between. He or she handles the financial negotiations, which may last for months. In some segments of modern society, the services of the go-between are often dispensed with, and the families enter into direct negotiations.

Occasionally the man and woman are involved in the choice of their own marriage partner, but parental approval is still required. Once the negotiations are complete, several women from the groom's family go to the bride's house for the ceremony of promise. They are served tea and given sweets on a tray that they take home with them. That tray is sent back by the groom's family within the week, filled with money, and then the engagement is announced. Wedding gifts, consisting of jewelry

An engagement party in Kabul. The groom's mother throws candy over the heads of the happy couple to wish them all the best for their marriage.

and clothing, are delivered by women from the groom's family before the wedding takes place.

In the country a wedding lasts for three days, and most of the expenses are borne by the groom's family. The bride's entourage, but not the bride, goes to the groom's home on the first day of the wedding to socialize and to get to know his family. The next day the groom leads a procession on a horse, with musicians and dancers to announce his arrival. Rifles are fired at intervals during the procession. The festivities continue on the third day with a feast, singing, and dancing at the groom's house; various games are played while the guests banter with the groom. In the evening, the procession picks up the bride at her home and winds back to the groom's house; this time the bride rides in the groom's car or in front of the groom on horseback.

The official ceremony, the *nikahnamah* (ni-KAH-naw-MAH), takes place on the third night. The *nikahnamah* is the signing of the marriage contract before witnesses. This ceremony ends with recitations from the Koran by the officiating mullah and the throwing of sugared almonds and walnuts onto the bridegroom.

In the cities the more Westernized Afghans no longer hold such long and elaborate weddings. They combine all the ceremonies so that the wedding lasts for only a day, with the rituals usually occurring at one of the popular restaurants. Most of the guests and even the groom wear Western dress; the bride is still likely to wear a traditional green or red velvet dress.

## CHILDREN

There is a great deal of rejoicing when a baby is born, especially if the baby is a boy. The celebrations may go on for as long as three days, with guns being fired, drums beaten, and food distributed to the poor.

On the third day the baby is named, usually by its paternal uncles. Among the more urbanized families, the parents choose the name. The mullah first whispers "*Allah-u-Akbar*" (God is great) in the baby's ear and then whispers its name. He also informs the baby about its ancestry and exhorts it to be a good Muslim and to uphold its family's honor.

Among the nomads the oldest paternal uncle gives the child its name and assumes a role similar to that of a godfather in Christian societies. He will be responsible for the child if the father dies.

The birth of a boy has greater significance because he will be an heir. He will be indoctrinated from a young age with the principles of *Pashtunwali* and expected to uphold the good name and honor of his family. Girls are usually not ill-treated, but their needs always come second to those of the males in the family, and they may even be neglected. All children are brought up in the women's quarters. The mother breast-feeds the child until the next baby comes or the child is too old.

Children are toilet-trained by their mothers when still very young and taught to feed themselves. It is the mother who must discipline the children; their fathers usually indulge them. However, it is the father who usually bathes and dresses his little sons.

The women in Afghanistan wield power in family affairs, and the participation of men in some family duties is seen as an example of women's influence. Men who are favored by the women of a household also have greater say in domestic matters.

In rural societies young boys learn to watch over the animals as they graze. Unlike in Western society, there is no marked adolescence. When a boy is about seven years old, he leaves the women's quarters and is circumcised, usually by an itinerant barber.

A feast is held, with games of physical skill and prizes of money or expensive turban cloth given to the victors by the boy's father. After this the boy is treated as a man; he is allowed to wear a turban or a cap and is expected to take care of himself. He must begin to help his father in the fields. A nomad child learns to ride and shoot, and watches the herds.

*Chadari*-clad women with their babies in Andkhoy.

No ceremony marks a girl's arrival at puberty, but in certain areas, especially Paktia province, molasses is distributed among the women as a special treat. The girls help look after their younger siblings and, like the boys, watch over the grazing herds. By the time they are about nine or ten, they have learned the skills to be a good wife and mother. They are able to grind wheat and corn, fetch water, cook, sew, clean, and make dung patties for fuel.

After decades of war the children of Afghanistan have suffered too. In many instances young boys have become the family breadwinner because the father has died in the war or from illness. In Kabul the street children earn a living for themselves and their families by shining shoes or washing cars. They may earn a dollar a day cleaning shoes and with that they buy the basics of bread and sugar for the family. Rice is a treat and meat is a luxury. The UN estimated that in 2011 there were 50,000 children on the streets in Kabul alone. It has also been estimated that 3 out of 10 children die before the age of 5 and half of all those who do survive are severely malnourished.

In 2011 the World Food Program delivered one high-energy biscuit a day to approximately 400,000 school children in some of the most remote and

poorest provinces in Afghanistan. The specially manufactured biscuits were intended to boost the nutrition levels of the children living in areas where the food source is unreliable. The biscuits are very popular with the children. The World Food Program's Food for Education program will help encourage parents to ensure the children attend school, knowing that they will get a snack that is highly nutritious.

The international community has spent billions of dollars over the last decade in an attempt to improve the lives of Afghans and rebuild the country. It has been recognized that children must have access to education and vocational training to secure their futures.

Children attending classes in Aq Robat, a remote village where families live a subsistence lifestyle, making the occasional journey to Bamian to sell excess crops whenever the harvest allows. The conditions there remain harsh with one of very few concrete buildings being the school, which was completed with the support of an international NGO.

## EDUCATION

Until the early 1900s the only education available was at mosque schools, which were attended only by boys. Girls acquired their religious training from elderly women, who conducted classes at home.

King Habibullah Khan founded the first modern school in Kabul, in 1903. He refuted opposition from the mullahs with the argument that providing an education was deemed an obligation by the Prophet Muhammad. He patterned the school on the Aligarh University in India and called it Habibia. Secular as well as Islamic subjects were taught. Habibia High School was totally destroyed during the civil war in the early 1990s. The school began to be reconstructed in 2004 after President Hamid Karzai, himself a former pupil, came to power. At present it has a capacity of 3,000 students.

King Habibullah also founded a military academy for army officers and a training college for teachers. Education made further rapid strides under the reign of King Habibullah's son and successor, King Amanullah, when a number of schools were opened in urban as well as some rural areas.

Habibia had by then become an academic high school patterned on the French secondary school system, and its first high school class graduated in 1923. Four more high schools were opened in Kabul and other major towns between 1923 and 1928. The first school for girls was opened in Kabul in 1921. Between 1921 and 1928 more than 800 girls attended this school in Kabul. The constitution of 1931 made primary education compulsory and free for all children. However, by 1940 there were still only 250 primary schools for boys, and even by 1967 the government had not succeeded in providing adequate facilities.

Girls studying at a school in Kabul.

After World War II, Afghanistan's educational system was greatly influenced by the United States, Britain, France, and Germany. During the 1950s more girls' schools were opened in spite of opposition from conservative Afghans. Progress in education was often slow because of poor attendance. In rural areas parents were reluctant to forgo their children's help in the fields, and many children could not attend school for several months during the winter because they could not get there. Moreover educating the children of nomads was difficult. Mobile schools and traveling teachers were introduced to address this problem.

Village schools are often run by a single person and modeled on the religious or mosque schools. The different languages spoken even in one area present a major problem. The official language of the school is the first language of the majority in the region. The Koran, however, is taught everywhere in Arabic.

By 1967 there were some 58 vocational schools offering courses in agriculture, technology, commerce, economics, arts and crafts, tailoring, secretarial services, and home economics. In addition there were special training programs in civil aviation, community development, accountancy and finance, radio operation, and nursing.

Although more Afghan children are attending school today, and efforts are being made to extend educational opportunities to the rural populations, in February 2005 Afghanistan's National Human Development Report stated that Afghanistan, with its unfortunate lack of teaching facilities and buildings, as well as a shortage of trained teaching professionals, has "the worst educational system" in the world.

Higher education began in 1931 with the founding of the College of Medicine at the new Kabul University. This was followed in the 1940s by the faculties of law, science, and literature. In 1947 Kabul University was formally established. Originally, as a concession to the conservative segments of society, separate departments of medicine, science, and letters were run for women. By 1960 all faculties were coeducational. In 2008 there were more than 9,000 students at the university and about 25 percent were women. In 2012 the Faculty of Computer Science celebrated the graduation of 68 students, including 20 female graduates.

During the Soviet occupation, of the 1.57 million school-age children in refugee camps, no more than 20 percent received formal education of any kind. Higher and secondary education was even more badly affected, as there were only about 145 high schools for hundreds of thousands of students. With only 78 primary schools for girls, their education was negligible. There remained a great deal of prejudice against educating girls. Most schools in the refugee camps were run by Christian organizations, and their influence was feared by parents.

The Afghan education system is currently being reconstructed. Decades of warfare destroyed most of the educational infrastructure. In 1996 the education and employment of women was totally prohibited. Before the ban women had accounted for 70 percent of the country's teachers. Education in Afghanistan improved from 2002 onward. According to estimates there were about 8 million children enrolled in schools by 2006, and nearly 35 percent were girls. However, in 2007, increased Taliban activity forced the closure of 35 percent of the schools in the southern provinces. In 2008 there were about 9,000 schools operating but the ratio of girls to boys was one to three or four.

In 2011 it was estimated that nearly 7 million children were enrolled in schools, and about 37 percent were girls. This was made possible by the construction or reconstruction of nearly 4,500 school buildings and an eight-fold increase in the number of teachers to 170,000. Out of 673 schools closed because of insurgency, 200 have been reopened, providing an education for 180,000 students and jobs for 3,000 teachers.

The Ministry of Education, with the support of its development partners, aims to ensure that Afghan children enjoy a bright future, planning to have

10 million children in school by 2015. There is a need to train teachers, print textbooks, and rebuild or renovate schools. In 2011 the Ministry allocated $5 million to send about 2,000 students abroad on higher education scholarships.

## REFUGEES

Afghanistan's extreme poverty, combined with continuing conflict, turmoil, and natural disasters, has left the majority of the population vulnerable and unable to cope. More than 5.7 million people have returned since the fall of the Taliban. In 2008 alone about 280,000 refugees returned. There are more than 450,000 internally displaced people in Afghanistan. Conflict in the two years from 2009 to 2011 led to more than 250,000 people fleeing their villages. Refugees are vulnerable and face an uncertain future. A drought in 2011 left an estimated 2.6 million people short of food.

Young children lining up for fresh drinking water in Kabul. With clean drinking water increasingly available, the overall health conditions in the country have improved.

## HEALTH CARE

Afghanistan's health indicators are near the bottom of international indices. Life expectancy is low (49 years for males and 52 years for females). There is high infant, under-five, and maternal mortality, at 121.63 per 1,000 live births, 191 per 1,000 live births, and 1,200 per 100,000 live births, respectively. Many Afghans are malnourished and there is widespread occurrence of micronutrient deficiency.

With help from the international community and the World Health Organization (WHO), the government is rebuilding and improving primary health care. Tuberculosis remains a serious health problem, and about 500 diagnostic centers have been established. The success rate in treatment was 90 percent in 2011. In 2008 more than 4 million cases of malaria were reported in Afghanistan. Rapid diagnostic tests have been introduced and long-lasting insecticide-treated mosquito nets have been provided free to the worst affected communities and provinces.

In a serious bid to improve health care and reduce infant and child mortality rates, health-care officials make trips to both urban and rural households to administer immunization against preventable diseases including polio and measles. Afghanistan is one of the remaining four polio-endemic countries in the world.

In 2000 it was estimated that 9 percent of the population had access to primary health-care services within two hours' walking distance. This deficiency was addressed with the assistance of the WHO and by 2006 that figure had increased to 65 percent of the population and by 2010 it was 90 percent of the population.

Elaborately carved graves in Afghanistan. When an Afghan dies, neighbors often send food and money, and lend emotional support.

## DEATH

When a Muslim is on his or her deathbed, family and friends gather around to recite verses from the Koran and lament. Often these expressions of sorrow can be very loud and dramatic, even though Islam advocates the acceptance of death as an act of Allah.

Once a man dies his male relations, with the help of the mullah (who recites prayers), bathe the body. Female relatives do this for a deceased woman. The ritual ablution, which is normally done in life before the daily prayers, is performed on the body. The toes are tied together, and the body is then shrouded in white cloth.

The body must be buried as soon as possible, but never at night. In the country it is taken to the mosque, where a prayer for the dead is said. In urban Afghanistan the body remains at home while a prayer service is held at the mosque. Occasionally this service is held at the graveside.

The grave must be about 6 feet (1.8 m) long and at least 2 feet (0.6 m) deep to allow the corpse to sit up on the Day of Judgment. The feet must point toward Mecca so that when the corpse sits up, it will face the holy city of Mecca. In some areas the body is buried on its right side, with the face toward Mecca.

Pottery or stone lamps are lighted on the grave, and for a year, prayers are said for the deceased every Thursday night. On the 14th and 40th days after the death of a person, close relatives and friends visit first the grave, to offer prayers, then the deceased's home, where the family will have prepared a meal. The same ritual is held after a year. On the first anniversary of the death, the women of the family, who have worn only white, the color of mourning, for that period, visit the gravesite to be released from mourning.

Many rituals and beliefs are throwbacks to the practices of pre-Islamic times. Head and foot markers on graves in Nuristan look very much like grave effigies from Kafir, or pre-Islamic, times. In Pashtun areas, a narrow white cloth is tied from the head to the foot of a grave. When this strip breaks it is believed that the soul has escaped to purgatory to await the Day of Judgment. It is also believed that the damned soul of an improperly buried person can return to kill or enslave other souls and can be controlled only by practitioners of black magic. Afghans never remove any plant from a graveyard, for this is believed to bring death to the family or release an evil spirit that may be imprisoned in the roots.

## INTERNET LINKS

**www.bbc.co.uk/news/world-south-asia-12936758**

This is a photographic slideshow from BBC news with captions and images of the restoration of Kabul Bazaar.

**www.aidafghanistan.net/mission.htm**

This is the official website of Aid Afghanistan for Education, the organization dedicated to empowering women and rehabilitating the education system in Afghanistan.

**www.ungei.org/news/afghanistan_2343.html**

This website contains information about education for girls in Afghanistan and the United Nations Girls' Education Initiative (UNGEI).

# RELIGION

The Friday Mosque of Herat, also known as the Jumah Mosque, was first built by the Timurids and then extended or passed down by several rulers, including the Safavids, the Mughals, and the Uzbeks.

# 8

TOGETHER WITH Christianity, Islam is one of the major religions of the world. Although the Middle East has traditionally been the stronghold of Islam, the religion also has hundreds of millions of adherents throughout the rest of the world.

Muslims are what Islam's followers are called. Islam was founded by the Prophet Muhammad in Mecca in the seventh century. Muhammad, according to tradition, received revelations from God through the angel Gabriel when he was about 40 years old. The word for "God" in Arabic, and as used throughout the Muslim world, is *Allah*. These revelations were compiled and written in the Koran and form the basis for the tenets of Islam. Islam shares some Judeo-Christian beliefs, such as the existence of only one God (in this case, Allah), the account of Abraham, and the angel Gabriel.

Afghanistan has been an Islamic state since 1992, when the various mujahideen groups succeeded in overthrowing the Soviet-backed President Buhannudin Rabbani. More than 99 percent of the population is Muslim. The country's small Hindu and Sikh population is estimated at fewer than 30,000. Sunni Muslims form approximately 80 percent of Afghans and the remainder, mostly Hazaras and Tajiks, are Shi'a Muslims. There are doctrinal disagreements between the Sunni and the Shi'a Muslims that influence events to this day.

Nevertheless Islam forms an extremely strong bond among the diverse peoples of this country. Their strong faith in their religion spurred the Afghans to withstand the Soviet onslaught. The tenets and beliefs of Islam guide its adherents in any given situation, whether personal, social, economic, or political.

In the eighth century all of the Prophet Muhammad's known sayings, decisions, and responses to various life situations, and to philosophical and legal questions, were brought together in the Sunnah (SOON-nah). The Sunnah, commonly referred to as the "Prophet's traditions," forms the second source of the Islamic faith and law after the Koran.

Islam not only dictates the religious observances and rituals but also lays down laws for almost all aspects of everyday life. Because of this, the mullahs have held extensive power over much of the Afghan lifestyle for centuries.

The increase in secular education and greater urbanization in the 20th century eroded some of the mullahs' influence. However, with the mujahideen groups now in power, Islam can be expected to take on an even greater role in every Afghan's life.

A large majority of Afghans are Muslim. Here in Uruzgan, Afghan men pray at one of the main mosques.

## THE FIVE PILLARS OF ISLAM

Islam imposes five main obligations, or pillars, on its followers. These laws are written down in the Koran—the basic source of Islamic teachings.

**SHAHADAT** The most important principle of Islam is the belief that God (Allah) is the one and only deity and that Muhammad is God's prophet or messenger. This, the first pillar of Islam, is called the *Shahadat* (sheh-hah-DEHT). Anyone who converts to Islam must take an oath that on the Day of Judgment he or she will bear witness to this belief.

It is the duty of every Muslim to visit the holy city of Mecca in Saudi Arabia at least once in his or her lifetime, unless prevented from doing so by reason of poverty or illness.

**SALAT** This refers to prayers, which form the second pillar. After ritual washings, a Muslim must pray five times a day, facing toward Mecca, Islam's holy city. The prayers must be said at dawn, immediately after noon, in the late afternoon, at dusk, and at night. The faithful are called to these prayers by the muezzin (moo-EZ-in), using the call to prayer known as the *Azan*. The prayer may be performed alone by the individual or with the congregation in a mosque. Praying in a mosque is more common for Muslim men than women. Women who go to the mosque must pray in an area set aside for them. Friday can be considered the Muslim Sabbath, although they do not call it that. All must gather for the noon prayer at the mosque, and a sermon is delivered by the religious leader of that community or by an Islamic scholar.

**ZAKAT** Every Muslim must give a certain percentage of his personal wealth to the poor each year. This is usually done in the month of Ramazan (RAM-ah-ZAHN), called Ramadan (RAM-ah-DAHN) in other parts of the Muslim world. This is the month when Muslims fast. The payment, or *zakat* (zeh-KAHT), may be made directly or indirectly, through the clergy or the government. In Afghanistan the traditional amount is 2.5 percent of one's annual income. This act is believed to purify a Muslim's possessions.

**SAWM** During the month of Ramazan, the ninth month of the Muslim calendar, no food or drink may be consumed between dawn and dusk. The act of fasting is called *sawm*. The dawn meal, called *sahari*, is eaten to sustain the individual until dusk, when the fast is broken with the evening meal, known as *iftar* (if-TAAR). In most towns and villages the times for these meals are announced from the mosque. In Kabul the cannon on Sher Darwaza Hill is fired an hour before sunrise so that people can wake up and eat. The second time the cannon is fired, all eating must cease. At dusk the cannon is again fired to announce the end of the fasting.

**HAJJ** The hajj is the pilgrimage to Mecca in Saudi Arabia, where the Kaaba, believed by Muslims to be the House of Allah on earth, was built by Abraham at Allah's command. On the 9th day of the 12th month of the Islamic calendar, the pilgrim must perform set rituals and prayers at the Kaaba and in other strategic places in its vicinity. The next day animals are slaughtered as a sacrifice to Allah and to commemorate the slaying of a sheep by Abraham, in place of his son, at Allah's command.

## SHI'A AND SUNNI

After the death of the Prophet Muhammad in A.D. 632, there was disagreement over his successor and his followers split into two groups. The Sunni, or Sunnite Muslims, believed that his successor should be elected from among the prophet's companions. The Shi'a, or Shi'ite Muslims, believed that the Prophet had appointed his son-in-law and cousin, Hazrat Ali, as his successor.

There are similarities and differences between the Koran and the Bible. The Koran recognizes a line of prophets, including Moses and the prophets of the Old Testament, but Muslims believe Muhammad is the last in the line. The Koran affirms the existence of angels as God's messengers, like the Bible. However, it also mentions jinns, or spiritual beings created from fire. Rebellious jinns are called demons, and Satan is believed to be the chief demon.

Over the centuries, other differences between the Sunni and Shi'a evolved, but the original dispute over the succession to the Prophet Muhammad remains the most crucial of the differences. Today approximately 90 percent of the world's estimated 1.57 billion Muslims are Sunni. Of the total Muslim population, 10 to 13 percent are Shi'a Muslims and 87 to 90 percent are Sunni Muslims. Most Shi'as (between 68 percent and 80 percent) live in just four countries—Iran, Pakistan, India, and Iraq.

## PRE-ISLAMIC BELIEFS

The religious beliefs of rural Afghan Muslims are still mixed with the superstitions and rituals of their pre-Islamic past. Most villagers believe in the influence of good and bad spirits and try to placate them. Jinns, mentioned in the Koran as spiritual beings, are thought to threaten women and children with evil. Amulets and talismans are acquired and worn for protection against the jinns.

The Sunni Muslims believe that Hazrat Ali is buried in Mazar-i-Sharif. The name *Mazar-i-Sharif* means "Noble Shrine" or "Tomb of the Exalted." The Shi'a Muslims believe that Hazrat Ali is buried in Najaf, Iraq.

There are numerous shrines, or tombs of saintly persons, in Afghanistan. Women, especially, go to these to receive blessings or to ask for special favors. To make a wish or to swear vengeance, a piece of colored cloth is tied to a stick buried near the shrine.

## NON-MUSLIMS

Non-Muslims make up a very small portion of Afghanistan's population—just one percent. They are predominantly urban dwellers. Despite their small numbers, Sikhs, Hindus, and Jews have played leading roles in the country's commercial life. Many have contributed much to the socioeconomic well-being of the country and brought about much progress in many sectors that had been left untapped and undeveloped due to war and militancy.

A small community of Parsis, who are Zoroastrians originally from Persia, has remained in Afghanistan. But of other older religions, such as Buddhism, that had strong connections in ancient times, nothing remains.

## INTERNET LINKS

**www.fas.org/irp/crs/RS21745.pdf**

This document written by Christopher M. Blanchard, an analyst in Middle Eastern affairs, describes the historical background, core beliefs, and shared practices of Sunni Islam and Shi'ite Islam.

**www.pewforum.org/Muslim/Mapping-the-Global-Muslim-Population.aspx**

This Pew Forum website provides detailed information on world religions and public life. It includes statistics and also has a link to a report on the size and distribution of the world's Muslim population.

**http://sacredsites.com/asia/afghanistan/mazari_sharif.html**

This website provides information and photographs on Mazar-i-Sharif and the Blue Mosque.

# LANGUAGE

A young girl reads her textbook at a school in Afghanistan.

## 9

A FGHANISTAN'S MANY ETHNIC groups speak a great variety of languages. The two most important languages are Pushtu (also spelled Pashtu), the language of the Pashtuns, the largest group in the country, and Dari, a language similar to Persian. Both Pushtu and Dari are official languages in Afghanistan, and most Afghans will understand at least one or the other in addition to their mother tongue.

Many of Afghanistan's languages, including Pushtu and Dari, have a common root in the Indo-European language family. According to estimates, about 35 percent of Afghans speak Pushtu and about 50 percent speaks Dari. The Pashtuns, Tajiks, Hazaras, Aimaq, Baluchis, and Nuristanis speak Dari or Pushtu. The other major language family in Afghanistan is Turkic, which is spoken by the Uzbeks, Turkomans, Kyrgyzs, and other Turkish groups. Turkic languages predominate in the northern regions and are spoken by about 11 percent of the people.

## THE INDO-EUROPEAN LANGUAGES

The Indo-European group of languages includes the languages of Iran, India, and Pakistan, as well as most of Europe. Scholars believe that the Indo-European languages were brought to these sites by Aryan invaders about 3,000 years ago. All the different languages of the Indo-European family have the same structure, and many of the words in their vocabularies sound similar as they stem from the same linguistic matrix.

Most Pashtuns speak Pushtu. The Tajiks and some of the urban Pashtuns speak Dari. The Hazaras use Hazaragi, which is a dialect of Dari. The distribution of dialects and languages forms a pattern related to the different geographical regions. In the southwestern plateau Pushtu predominates. In the northern plains and central highlands Dari, Uzbek, and Turkic are spoken, whereas in the northeastern region Dari and the various languages of the Dardic branch of the Indo-European family enjoy wider usage.

Dari is often used for communication between different groups because most Afghans speak it. In the 1930s, during the reign of Zahir Shah, the government tried to promote the use of Pushtu. For example, in 1936, Pushtu was declared the national language of Afghanistan. Dari, however, prevailed because of its importance in literature and because it is the language most used by the business community of the country.

Various ancient Indo-European languages are spoken by small communities living in the Pamir Knot region in Badakhshan and in the Pamir Mountains. Among the more important groups are the Shughnis, the Wakhis, and the Munjis. Each local variant may have only a few thousand speakers.

*Elderly men gather to chat in Helmand. The languages used in Afghanistan are mainly Pushtu and Dari (Afghan Persian).*

## SHARED LANGUAGES

Most of the languages spoken in Afghanistan are also used in neighboring countries. Besides Dari, which shares its roots with Farsi, spoken in Iran, Uzbek and Turkic are spoken in the Central Asian republics of the former Soviet Union. Many Pakistanis also speak Pushtu, and Baluchi is common to the Baluchis who live in Afghanistan, Iran, Turkmenistan, and Pakistan. Tajiki is the Persian dialect spoken in Tajikistan and in parts of Uzbekistan. Khorasani, spoken by Persian speakers in the west and to the north of Kabul, is yet another Dari dialect.

The main Dari dialect found in Afghanistan is Kabuli, which is used by the majority of the educated elite. The structure of the Aimaq language is Iranian, but its vocabulary borrows heavily from Turkic languages. Hazaragi, spoken by the Hazaras, is a Dari dialect too, but also contains many Turkic and Mongol words. Hazaragi is also spoken in Iran and Pakistan.

Punjabi and Sindhi are the main Indian languages spoken in Afghanistan by Hindus and Sikhs in the urban centers of eastern Afghanistan. Hindu merchants sometimes use Urdu as a language of trade.

Afghans browsing at a makeshift roadside book stall in Helmand.

All the different languages are again divided into dialects, each with a different pronunciation and vocabulary. Except in the case of extreme dialectical variation, most people speaking the same language can understand its dialects. Afghans who are not native Dari speakers, for example, usually know enough of the language to communicate with those speaking other languages.

## SCRIPT

The many languages found in Afghanistan have a common factor: they are all written in the same Arabic script, from right to left. The Arabic characters are supplemented, as needed, by the addition of diacritical marks to represent sounds that do not exist in Arabic. Because so many languages in Afghanistan are related, anyone who has learned the expanded alphabet can read the script of these languages.

## FOREIGN LANGUAGES

English, French, German, Italian, and Russian are spoken by some of the educated Afghans because these languages were taught in some schools before the Taliban regime. The literate among the Afghans can often speak

*Afghans use a great deal of body language to express themselves. There is also substantial physical contact among members of the same sex. Any touching between opposite sexes is strictly forbidden, in keeping with Islamic doctrine. When greeting friends and acquaintances, to express warmth and camaraderie, Afghan men often clasp both hands in a firm handshake, hugging and kissing each other on the cheeks. Unlike in Western countries, they do not feel self-conscious walking arm-in-arm with other men. In business dealings, contracts or agreements are sealed with a firm nodding of the head.*

not only a couple of other Afghan dialects besides their mother tongue, but also a few non-Afghan languages. It is not uncommon to meet officials who can speak as many as four or five languages, including English and Urdu.

## THE PRESS IN AFGHANISTAN

The first newspaper in Afghanistan was published in the middle of the 19th century during the reign of Ameer Sher Ali. The Persian-language *Kabul*, later known as *Shams-un-Nahar*, published the latest happenings at the royal courts and lasted until 1879.

After World War I Amanullah Khan had used the press to popularize his modernization campaign, and during his reign, no fewer than 15 newspapers were in circulation. The first daily newspaper, *Afghan*, was published in Kabul in 1920. By the 1950s newspapers in Kabul had special Friday editions, which included short stories and poetry. The Ministry of Information and Culture launched an English-language newspaper in 1962. The *Kabul Times* included domestic and international news. Under the liberal Press Law of 1965 the newspapers flourished until 1973 and the formation of the republic, under which there was more control of opposition newspapers.

The government-owned press became a source of communist propaganda after the Soviet invasion in 1978. At this time, and also during the subsequent Taliban administration, there were rigidly enforced media laws controlling the newspapers that could be published. Foreign magazines and newspapers were not permitted.

Since the overthrow of the Taliban, the media in Afghanistan have started to flourish. Many new publications have been launched, including several for women. In 2002 the *Kabul Weekly* was finally published again after five years of silence. In 2010 there were 27 daily newspapers and 48 weekly newspapers published, mostly funded by international aid or political parties. The government needs wide press coverage to get its messages across to a people who are widely divided not only geographically but also culturally and politically. The new laws on freedom of the press are quite lenient, but communications infrastructure is very rudimentary, at least 60 percent of the population is illiterate, and it is estimated that only 2.5 out of every 100 Afghans read newspapers.

## INTERNET LINKS

**www.ethnologue.com/show_country.asp?name=afghanistan**

This is the web version of the comprehensive reference volume that catalogs all the known living languages in the world today, especially for Afghanistan.

**http://worldpress.org/newspapers/ASIA/Afghanistan.cfm**

This is one of the web's largest and most comprehensive directories of world newspapers and magazines, sorted by country. There are links to all the newspapers and magazines listed.

**www.afghanistan.culturalprofiles.net/?id=-114**

This website contains information about Afghanistan cultural policy and infrastructure with links to arts, archives, libraries, broadcasting, internet, press, and publishing.

**www.nato.int/docu/review/2011/Afghanistan-2011/Afghan-blogger/EN/index.htm**

This *NATO Review Magazine* website contains links to many articles on contemporary Afghanistan.

The move toward freedom of speech began as soon as it was learned that Kabul was liberated on November 13, 2001, and that the Taliban regime had been toppled. Jamila Mujahed, the best-known female broadcaster in Afghanistan, was woken up by some journalists and members of the Northern Alliance. Without hesitation, she rushed to the studio in the midst of the fighting. Most of the transmitters had been destroyed by the U.S. bombing campaign. Using an old, weaker transmitter, she made the historic and much-awaited announcement, "Dear fellow citizens of Kabul, the Taliban have fled Kabul."

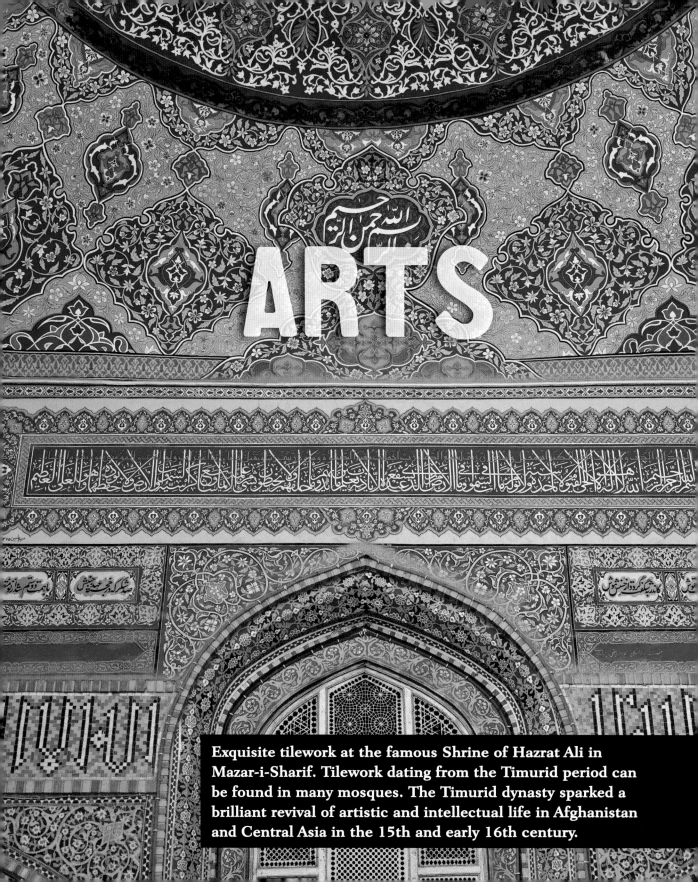

# ARTS

Exquisite tilework at the famous Shrine of Hazrat Ali in Mazar-i-Sharif. Tilework dating from the Timurid period can be found in many mosques. The Timurid dynasty sparked a brilliant revival of artistic and intellectual life in Afghanistan and Central Asia in the 15th and early 16th century.

# 10

A FGHANISTAN HAS A RICH CULTURAL heritage covering over 5,000 years. Archaeological research carried out since 1992 has uncovered many exceptional works of art from the Islamic and pre-Islamic periods. Traditional art forms have been revived and there is a new enthusiasm in response to years of suppression.

Some artists are inspired by the Herat School of the 15th century Timurid period, while others are influenced by modern and contemporary Western styles.

## PRE-ISLAMIC HERITAGE

Small clay statues from the Neolithic period have been found in Afghanistan. These may have been considered protective divinities. Notable archaeological findings include the rock and pillar edicts of Ashoka the Great, which were erected to preach Buddhism and encourage pacifism by his subjects, and the ruins of the ancient Greek city at Ai Khanoum, thought to be the ruins of the city of Alexandria on Oxus, founded in 329 B.C. Excavations of the ruins show that they were built on an earlier Persian site. It was in ancient Afghanistan that the artistic and architectural styles of the Greeks, Buddhists, and the Indus River civilizations fused to yield the Greco-Buddhist and Gandhara schools of art. Ancient Afghan art treasure was discovered in the interior of Buddhist stupas. The treasure of Bagram, dating from the 1st and 2nd centuries A.D., was discovered in 1937—39 and contained glassware, bronze statuettes and vessels, and plaster casts of Hellenistic

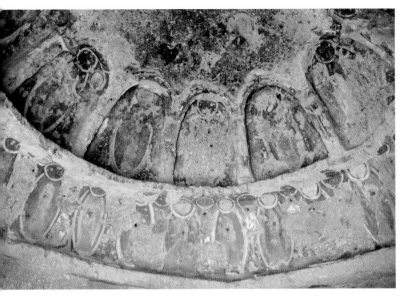

themes. These objects came from the Mediterranean world. The treasure also contained a carved wooden piece of furniture decorated with ivory. This originated from central India. Chinese lacquer bowls were also discovered and these testify to the use of the Silk Route through modern Afghanistan.

## ISLAMIC HERITAGE

Afghanistan has played an important role in the development of Islamic culture in general. The greatest progress was made during the Ghaznavid era of the 10th and 11th centuries and the Timurid era of the 14th and 15th centuries.

Mahmud of Ghazni (971—1030) summoned renowned men of learning to his court. Among those who came was Avicenna, a physician, scientist, and philosopher. Avicenna is famous for his book *Canon of Medicine*, which was used in medical schools in Europe before the 17th century. He also wrote many books on mathematics and astronomy. Also at Mahmud's court were 400 poets; among them was Firdausi, who composed the great epic *Shahnama* (*Book of Kings*). Mahmud and his successors also built magnificent mosques, palaces, and tombs.

The second great period of cultural development was at Herat under the Timurid rulers. Tamerlane and his successors ordered the construction of magnificent mosques and shrines. At Herat, Tamerlane established an elegant center of arts and learning.

## ARCHITECTURE

Timurid architecture is characterized by its tall minarets, bulbous domes, and colorful tiles and is considered by scholars to be among the best in the world. Outstanding examples of such architecture found today include the Friday Mosque in Herat and the Blue Mosque at Mazar-i-Sharif.

Buddhist frescoes discovered in the caves of Bamian. Buddhism, the religion founded by Gautama Buddha in India in the sixth century B.C. was first introduced in Afghanistan by rulers of the Mauryan Empire. Unfortunately, many of these frescoes were destroyed by the Taliban in 2001.

The Blue Mosque was built in A.D. 1420 by Amir Hussein and is said to contain the remains of Ali, the son-in-law of the Prophet Muhammad. The dome is of pristine simplicity, in sharp contrast to the lushly patterned walls. The architecture consists of sharp, clear forms, and the entrance is through imposing portals that lead into an extensive courtyard. The entire building is enhanced by contrasting forms and textures. To cover the walls, pieces of glazed tiles, in lapis lazuli, turquoise, deep green, yellow, black, and white, were carefully cut and fitted to form mosaic patterns of curving stems, leaves, and blossoms. Workmanship is so skilled that the panels appear to be painted, and the undulating surface causes the highly polished tiles to sparkle at certain angles.

Tile makers experienced in this ancient art still live in Afghanistan today and, in times of peace, have been employed in restoration works.

*The Shrine of Hazrat Ali, also known as the Blue Mosque, in Mazar-i-Sharif (meaning "Tomb of the Exalted"). It is one of the reputed burial places of Ali, the cousin and son-in-law of Muhammad.*

## LITERATURE

Afghanistan's literary heritage is among the richest in Central Asia. Herat was a renowned center for literary pursuit. The famous Persian language poet Jami settled there, as had the Arabic language author al-Hamadhani before him. Novels are rare in Afghan literature. Poetry, however, is highly revered and popular in Afghanistan, and each ethnic group has its own poetry, epics, and songs. These were usually transmitted orally from generation to generation, sometimes by performers who went from village to village entertaining the patrons of teahouses and *caravanserais*.

*Former prime minister Nur Mohammad Taraki had a growing reputation as a novelist until his entry into Afghan politics.*

*The poignant romance of Leila, the daughter of a nomadic chief, and the poet Qais bin Amir, called Majnun—the name* Majnun *means "Mad One" because his love cost him his sanity—has been told many times by poets, both as oral folklore and as literature. It is one of the most popular love stories, from Turkey all the way to the Malay archipelago in Southeast Asia.*

*In one version of the story, after Majnun has been driven mad by his love for Leila, his father approaches Leila's father to arrange a marriage between Leila and his son but is refused because Majnun is crazy. Leila ventures out in search of the wandering Majnun and is seen by Ibn Salam, a prince whom her father has committed her to marry. The prince imprisons Leila, but she escapes and finds Majnun. Realizing he cannot marry her because of his illness, Majnun sends his beloved back, and she dies in grief. A brokenhearted Majnun dies embracing her gravestone and is buried beside her.*

The most popular theme in Afghan literature is warfare, followed by love and jealousy, then religion and folklore. Most stories express a religious sentiment, besides extolling such virtues as courage.

Pashtun literature extols the warrior who dies for his principles. There are also many religious works written in Pushtu, such as the *Makhzanul-Asrar* and the *Makhzanul-Islam*. Khushal Khan Khattak (1613—89) and Abdur Rahman, who lived in the 17th century, are the most important Pushtu poets. Khushal Khan Khattak is considered the national poet of Afghanistan and has also written books on philosophy, ethics, medicine and an autobiography. He is held in awe by the Afghans because he was not only a great poet but also a warrior. Although constantly at war with the Moghuls or with other Pashtuns, Khattak wrote masterful poetry about war, love, and life.

Baluchi poetry paints vivid pictures of the Baluchi countryside and way of life, and nature is a favorite theme. Ideals, such as generosity, are exalted and greed condemned.

Turkic literature is shared by all its diverse groups. The magically swift horse, the faithful companion, and a hero possessing superhuman qualities are very common themes. Some of their epics that have become a shared

## CRITICIZING RELIGIOUS BIGOTRY

*The knowing, the perceptive man*
*Is he who knows about himself,*
*For in self-knowledge and insight*
*Lies knowledge of the Holiest.*
*If in his heart there is no fear,*
*His deeds are not those of the good,*
*Pay no heed to one who's skilled*
*In quoting the Koran by heart.*

*—A poem by Khushal Khan Khattak*

heritage are the Uzbek *Alpamysh*, which tells the story of the courage and bravery of Uzbek athletes, and *Batyr-Koblandy*, an epic poem about the life and victories of the Steppe warriors—the Batyrs.

Persian literature is the most widely memorized and recited body of work throughout Afghanistan. It is well known to the educated Afghans, and their odes and ballads have been transmitted orally through the generations. Children are told tales from *Kalilah wa Dimnah*, a collection of animal stories very like Aesop's fables, which were adapted and translated into Arabic from the Pahlavi in the eighth century by Ibn al-Muqaffa'. Also popular are tragic love stories, similar to Shakespeare's *Romeo and Juliet*; the most famous of these are *Leila and Majnun*, *Adam and Durkhani*, *Farhad and Shirin*, and *Yusof and Zulekha*.

Contemporary prose and poetry are written in Dari and often imitate the classical Persian style and format. In 1947 a literary-political society called Awakening Youth was formed, and, for a time, there was a period of greater freedom of expression among authors.

Afghan literature hails from much earlier Persian and Pashto traditions but contemporary Afghan writers often reflect paradoxes of location and culture. Homira Qaderi writes stories about Herat province in Dari. She lives in Tehran and her readership is mostly non-Afghan. Khaled Hosseini,

When Khushal Khan Khattak died in 1694, he left behind a considerable body of work, and many of his poems have since been translated by Pushtu scholars. Khushal Khan Khattak's grandson, Afdal Khan, later wrote a history of the Pashtuns.

living in California, is more famous abroad than in Afghanistan. The film adaptation of his first novel, *The Kite Runner*, was banned by the Kabul government in 2008 because of its depictions of ethnic conflict.

## VISUAL ARTS

Artists in Afghanistan were greatly influenced by the works of Kamaluddin Behzad (1450—1535), from the Timurid period in Herat. The Herat school of manuscript illumination developed a miniature style combining great technical skill with studied naturalism. Paintings consisted of precise and clear shapes in brilliant colors. Human, animal, and cloud forms were stylized, creating a tapestry-like effect.

A brightly decorated truck in Afghanistan. Afghan folk art often expresses a mood rather than attempting realistic imagery.

For many years Afghan art was ruled by Realism and dominated by men. The accuracy with which a young man could copy from a picture was the yardstick by which art was judged. An exceptional and talented artist was Abdul Ghaffour Breshna (1907—74). His work as a painter, composer, musician, and poet affected the development and renewal of Afghan art in the 20th century. He became a teacher, and later the director of the college of arts and crafts in Kabul, introducing new understanding and drawing techniques. Among his art students were Khair Mohammed, Professor Ghausuddin, Hafizullah, and Abdurrab, all of whom became famous in their own right.

Three decades of war and civil unrest stifled artists even further, and the formal study of any of the arts at the university level was considered a waste of time because a fine arts degree would not lead to a job. In the 1990s, under the Taliban, art was limited to calligraphy and the drawing of immortal shapes. However, in 2008, Kabul University hosted an exhibition on the themes of environment and pollution. All of the participating artists were women and the genre was modern art.

# THEATER AND MOVIES

Original Persian plays, and those adapted from European classics or Arabic and Turkish comedies, are performed at the few surviving theaters in Kabul, Herat, and Kandahar. Traveling companies take plays to the provincial towns and perform at local fairs.

Women's roles are often played by men, and most actors are amateurs. Among the European classics, the adaptations of Molière's comedies are very popular. Occasionally Shakespeare's plays are also adapted.

The Goethe-Institut in Kabul holds puppet theater workshops. The first puppetry workshop was held in July 2007 with 14 students from the University of Kabul, College of Fine Arts as well as eight members of the Mobile Mini Circus for Children (MMCC). As a result of this initiative, Parwaz was founded in 2009, the first puppet theater ensemble in Afghanistan.

Movie theaters usually show Iranian or Indian movies, especially those in Hindi, and Pakistani movies. Cinema is a very popular form of entertainment and some of the theaters have been renovated or rebuilt.

## INTERNET LINKS

**http://atwar.blogs.nytimes.com/2010/08/06/women-and-modern-art-in-afghanistan/**

This site contains interesting information within an article entitled "Women and Modern Art in Afghanistan," with information about contemporary art courses at Kabul University and recent exhibitions.

**www.afghan-web.com/culture/poetry/poems.html#**

This website has a section on poetry, with links to English translations of some well-known Afghan poems originally written in Dari and Pushtu.

**www.heritageinstitute.com/zoroastrianism/balkh/AiKhanum.htm**

This website provides information on the Zoroastrian Heritage of Afghanistan, including links to photographs and information on Balkh and Ai Khanum.

LEISURE

An Afghan youth enjoying a swing at the playground. The fall of the Taliban marked the beginning of a new Afghan experience, one of hope and aspirations for the individual.

A FGHANS TAKE GAMES AND sports very seriously. Winning in sports is, to the Afghan, of the utmost importance since a match is not just a friendly joust but also a question of personal, tribal, and family honor.

Games are often held during festivals and celebrations and draw huge crowds of spectators. Kite flying is popular among Afghans.

## CHILDHOOD GAMES

Afghani children, even with the horror and turmoil of a civil war, have continued to pay traditional games. The Taliban banned toys such as

Afghan children playing a game of cricket in Kabul.

## 11

Since the fall of the Taliban in November 2001 the Afghan people have once again been able to enjoy their traditional leisure activities. Few places in the world have had the curtain of oppression fall so suddenly, and lift so suddenly. Afghans are once again able to delight in the simplest of pleasures, including the reinvigorated film industry, music, dance, and kite flying.

dolls, kites, and stuffed animals, but even so traditional games continued. The games are simple. Many are local variations of hide-and-seek or hopscotch. *Aaqab* ("Eagle") is a tag game—one child is an eagle and sits on a rock; other children are pigeons and stand in a safe area. The children leave the safe area and pretend to be pigeons pecking the ground for crumbs of food. The child who is the eagle leaves the rock and chases the other children. When the eagle touches a child, that child is then out of the game. Play continues until all the pigeons are out and then another eagle is chosen.

*Bujal Bazi* is a game resembling marbles but played with sheep or goat knuckle bones. There are lots of regional variations but the object of the game is to knock the opponent's knuckle bones out of a circle drawn in the dirt.

*San Chill Bazi* (pebble games) is a game for girls that resembles the Western game of jacks. Each player chooses five pebbles, four of which are thrown down. The remaining pebble is thrown up gently, and one of the four pebbles is picked up without losing the initial pebble. If successful in picking up all four pebbles, in the next round the child will attempt to pick up two pebbles together. This goes on until the child fails to pick up the required number of pebbles, and then it is the next person's turn. The first child who completes all the stages is the winner.

In rural Afghanistan a little girl's toy may be a crudely carved doll made by her father, and her brother may play with a slingshot. Childhood ends early in Afghanistan. Afghan children have few years in which to play because they are expected to help out with the chores.

## KITE FLYING

*Gudiparan Bazi*, which literally means "flying puppet" or "doll fighting," is the national pastime of kite-fighting that was banned by the Taliban as un-Islamic when that regime was in power. Kite flying in Afghanistan is a competitive sport, unlike the hobby that it is in other parts of the world. The kites come in different sizes and are essentially thin paper stretched over a frame of bamboo. Afghani kites do not have tails. An adhesive material is mixed with mushed rice and grounded glass to make a paste. This paste is then coated onto the kite string to make it abrasive. The kite string, in Afghanistan, is

always wire because it is stronger. Leather gloves are often worn by kite fliers to avoid injury to their hands from the sharp wire string. One has to sever the kite string or shred the kite belonging to the opponent to win. Two kites have to be airborne simultaneously and at close proximity to each other. The fight could last from as little as a split second up to as long as it took to rip the kite of the opponent or to cut its string. Once the loser of the kite fight loses his kite it becomes the possession of whoever manages to catch it. Kite flying is a dangerous sport, especially in urban areas where it is necessary to climb on to the flat rooftops in order to have the best view of the kites. It is mostly played by young men and boys.

Afghan boys fly kites in Kabul. This activity was banned under the Taliban regime.

## BUZKASHI

Banned under the Taliban, buzkashi is to Afghans what baseball is to Americans. It is immensely popular. The game is believed to have been developed in Central Asia and the plains of Mongolia. It plays a major role in the lives of the people of northern Afghanistan. For the farmer and the nomad, it serves as a reminder of a heroic ancestry. The game is often played by Afghans during the Nowruz (neh-ROHZ) festival in March. Only men participate in buzkashi.

*Buzkashi* literally means "grab the goat," but a calf may be used instead. The headless carcass of a goat is placed in a circle drawn on the ground in the center of a circle formed by two teams of horsemen. The idea is to grab the headless goat and carry it around corner posts before dropping it back into the circle. Teams have been known to consist of as many as 1,000 players in unofficial games. When the signal is given, the riders gallop to the center, and each tries to lift the carcass onto his horse. This is no easy task in the noisy midst of flailing hooves, slashing whips, and the weight of the carcass. Horse and rider move in perfect harmony and are a joy to watch. Despite the potentially dangerous situation, serious injuries seldom occur because the horses are extremely well trained. Excellent communication between rider and horse can help reduce the risk of serious injury.

Afghan horsemen take part in the traditional buzkashi game in Maimana. Buzkashi is, by far, the most exciting Afghan national sport.

Once the goat is on his saddle, the rider must then ride to a point 1 to 3 miles (1.61 to 4.82 km) away, then return to the starting point and drop off the goat where he picked it up. Only then is he said to have scored a goal. During all this time, the other riders try to snatch the goat away from him.

The horses, ridden by the master players, or *chapandaz* (CHAP-an-DAAZ), who control the game, must be trained for at least five years. The Afghan saying "Better a poor rider on a good horse than a good rider on a poor horse" demonstrates the respect riders give their Habash and Tatar horses, whom they revere. Riders are often sponsored by the most powerful members of a region. The game, and its outcome, may often mirror the balance of power between cities, regions, or warlords. Real-life disputes can be played out in the field and, perhaps, resolved.

Rules are laid down by the Afghan Olympic Federation, and two types of fouls have been introduced—hitting an opponent intentionally with one's whip and forcing him off his horse. Flagrant defiance of these rules means expulsion from the game, forcing the team to fall short by one man.

The official rules limit the duration of a game to an hour each with a 10-minute break at halftime. Official teams consist of no more than 10 players each. These rules are followed only at official games. Buzkashi played in Afghanistan, especially those in the north, is as full of thrills and spills as ever and matches have been known to last up to a week.

## PAHLWANI AND OTHER SPORTS

Most games native to Afghanistan are violent and vigorous. Wrestling, or *pahlwani* (pahl-wah-NEE), is popular with men all over the country. The rules are simple—the wrestler may grab the arms or the clothing of his opponent but must not touch his legs. Usually wrestlers seize their opponent's forearms and move sideways in a crablike, rocking motion, trying to catch their adversary off-balance.

A *pahlwani* match in Kabul.

A man will leap high to try to toss his opponent, who in turn will twist in midair, ending behind the other man and holding him in a headlock. When one wrestler has been thrown to the ground and his shoulders have been pinned down, the winner is lifted waist-high by his coach and carried around the field to the cheers of the jubilant crowd.

In Nuristan the men and boys play a game resembling rugby. The two teams each stand in a row, one row of players facing the other. One man from each team tries to dash past the opposing team, whose players try to block him. This body-shaking game consists of a great deal of pushing and tripping.

King Habibullah, during his reign from 1901 to 1919, introduced Western sports such as tennis, golf, and cricket, and built several golf courses in Afghanistan. After World War II other team sports were introduced, including soccer. Their spirit of preserving honor enables the Afghans to excel at such games as basketball, soccer, volleyball, and field hockey.

## MUSIC AND DANCING

Music is an integral part of Afghan culture and traditions. Culturally Afghan music is cheerful and part of national and individual pride. In the evenings, young men often get together to sing and to play music. Afghans sing even while they work or travel. Although musicians are not well respected, it is socially acceptable for Afghans to play music for their own entertainment. Performances of Indian music are well patronized in the cities.

The music of the mountains is purely Afghan—simple yet vigorous, resembling the flamenco music of Spain. In the cities the songs have a strong Indian influence and also often reflect Western trends. Afghan music commonly takes the form of a song with lyrics but there is also a significant repertoire of purely instrumental music.

Although different in many aspects, Afghan music is closer to Western music than to any other music in Asia. Their orchestra consists of a number of string instruments, drums, and a small hand-pumped harmonium.

Attan is a traditional Afghan dance with variations according to ethnic and geographic divisions. It usually involves men performing a ritual dance accompanied by a *dhol*, which is a double-headed barrel drum with a very low and deep resonance. Other instruments can include a single-barreled *dhol*, tablas, the 18-stringed robab, surnai flute, and toola flute made of wood. The basic technique behind the Attan has not changed over the centuries. It is a circular dance performed by anywhere from two to more than a hundred people. The performers follow each other going round and round in a circle to the beat as the rhythm and beats faster.

Men dance at weddings and festivals. They usually dance with their swords and guns, in ever-widening circles. Older men form an inner circle, with the younger men in the middle, and horsemen dance on the outside. The music starts on a slow beat and picks up tempo as the dance progresses, until music and dancers reach a frenzy. The music then stops abruptly. After a short break, the dancing and music begin again. During Pashtun weddings, men and women dance in rows of 10 to 12 people, each waving a brightly colored scarf above the head. Apart from weddings, women usually dance when no men are present.

Nuristanis play a form of field hockey using a stick with a cylindrical, bulbous head. This game is often played on rooftops 30 feet (9 m) high, and although the players seldom fall off, it can look very precarious to spectators.

## INTERNET LINKS

**www.ehow.com/list_6128629_afghan-traditional-kids-games.html**

This website provides information on a number of traditional Afghan children's games and how they are played.

**www.foreignpolicy.com/articles/2010/01/29/afghanistans_ultimate_sport#7**

This photo essay from *Foreign Policy* shows the game of buzkashi—Afghanistan's national sport.

**www.easternartists.com/DANCE%202%20Afghan.html**

This site provides detailed information on the different traditional dances of Afghanistan, with additional information on the music and instruments used.

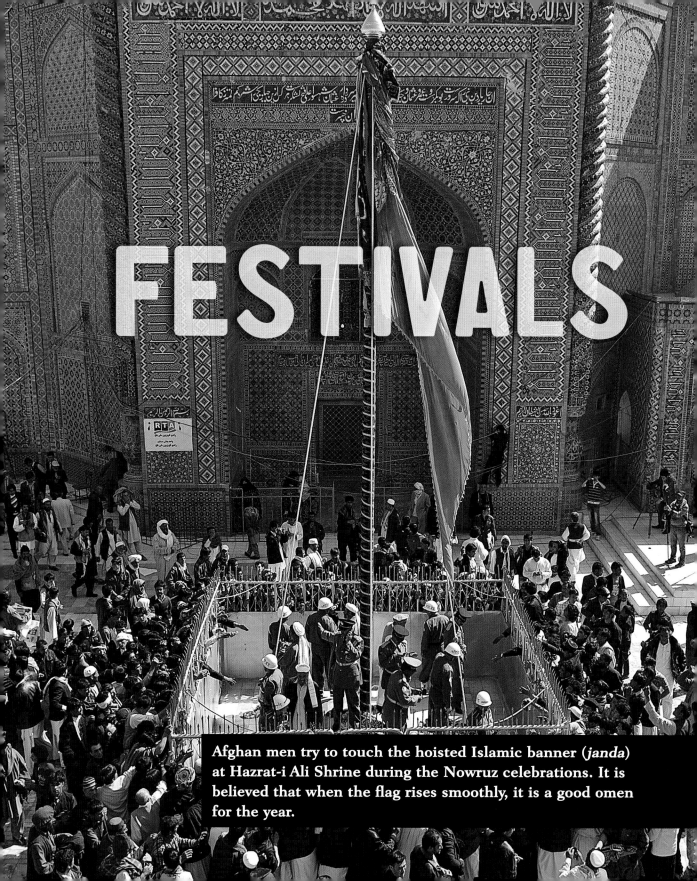

# FESTIVALS

Afghan men try to touch the hoisted Islamic banner (*janda*) at Hazrat-i Ali Shrine during the Nowruz celebrations. It is believed that when the flag rises smoothly, it is a good omen for the year.

## 12

AS IN MOST OTHER MUSLIM countries, many holidays in Afghanistan celebrate important events in the Islamic calendar. These holidays are usually marked with special prayers and sermons in mosques. Many Afghans also take the opportunity to visit relatives or entertain with lavish meals.

Independence Day in August and Revolution Day in April are the two most important secular holidays in Afghanistan.

## EID AL-FITR

The most important month in the Islamic calendar is Ramazan, the ninth month, during which every Muslim, except the old, the sick, young children, and pregnant women, is required to abstain from food, drink, smoking cigarettes or cigars, and chewing tobacco from dawn to dusk.

Fasting during Ramazan is called *sawm*, or *rozah*, in Afghanistan. Before dawn Muslims eat a meal called the *sehri* and fasting begins at sunrise. Most Afghans break their daily fast by eating dates or raisins before their customary evening meal and tea. The observance of fasting is important and reflects the obedience of a believer of Allah. *Sawm* teaches self-control and abstinence from material wants.

Following the Islamic lunar calendar instead of the traditional Afghan solar calendar, Ramazan occurs 11 days earlier each year; fasting can be arduous when it falls in the summer. The exact dates of Islamic holidays cannot be determined in advance because they are dependent on the

Children wait for their turn on a carnival ride on the first day of the Muslim holiday of Eid al-Fitr in Kabul.

expected visibility of the *hilal* (waxing crescent moon following a new moon). This also varies according to location. During Ramazan all activity slows down during the day, and the people liven up only after dusk falls.

The feast of *Eid al-Fitr* (EED AHL-fitr) commences the day after the month of fasting ends, on the first day of the month of *Shawal*. Celebrations usually last for three days. Congregational prayers are recited in mosques, after which Afghans visit their friends and relatives. New clothes, especially for the children, are made, and much food is prepared.

## EID AL-ADHA

Once the fasting month and ensuing celebrations have ended, it is time for those planning to perform their obligatory pilgrimage to Mecca to start preparations for their journey. The hajj, or pilgrimage, takes place in the 12th month of the Muslim calendar, the rituals being performed in Mecca between the 7th and the 10th days. Those who have made the pilgrimage are referred to, respectfully, as hajji (HAW-jee), if they are male, and *hajjah* (HAW-jah), if female.

A feast known as *Eid al-Adha* (EED AHL-ad-ah) in the Muslim world is celebrated on the 10th day of the 12th month. *Eid al-Adha* is the Feast of the Sacrifice. Animals, such as sheep, goats, and camels, are sacrificed, especially by those who have already performed the hajj. This act commemorates Abraham's faith, his obedience, and his love for Allah, and honors his willingness to offer his son as a sacrifice. Having passed the test of his faith, Abraham was stopped before the offering was made and at Allah's command a lamb was slayed and sacrificed instead.

One-third of the slaughtered animal is used by the family, another third is distributed to relatives, and the rest is given to the poor. This feast of the sacrifice is also referred to as *Qurbaan* (KOOR-bahn). In Turkic it is known as *Büyük Bairam* (boo-yook bai-RAHM).

## ASHURA

To the Shi'a, the most important religious period of the year is the first 10 days of the New Year. This is a period of mourning, in memory of the killing of Hussein, the grandson of the Prophet Muhammad, at Karbala on October 10 in A.D. 680, along with 72 of his immediate family and followers. The festival climaxes on the 10th day of the month of *Muharram* (MOO-har-ahm), called Ashura (ah-SHOO-rah).

Ashura is an optional fasting day. Because the Shi'a population is relatively small, this day is celebrated on a more modest scale in Afghanistan than in countries with large Shi'a populations, such as neighboring Iran. Mourners in Iran, for example, join a procession through the streets, giving themselves over to frenzied expressions of grief, beating themselves, and sometimes even drawing blood.

Afghan men and children play a game with boiled eggs on the second day of Eid al-Adha in Kabul.

## MAWLEED AL-NABI

Muslims also celebrate the birth of the Prophet Muhammad, who was born on the 12th day of the month of *Rabi-al-Awal* in A.D. 570. Mawleed al-Nabi is one of the most important holidays in Afghanistan, and prayers and feasting continue for weeks afterward. In homes, stories are told about Muhammad's life, his parents, and his birth. Religious leaders may also remind worshipers of their duties as Muslims.

The Prophet Muhammad is believed to have died on his birthday, adding significance to the importance and solemnity of the feast.

## NOWRUZ

Literally meaning "a new day," Nowruz (NO Rooz) is the first day of spring and New Year's Day on the Afghan solar calendar. It falls annually on March 21. This festival dates back to the time when Zoroastrianism was still a

*Eid al-Fitr,* pronounced "EED ahl-fitr" in Arabic, is also known as *Shaher-i-Bairam,* pronounced "shah-herh-REE-bai-RAHM," in Turkic, and *Qamqai Akhta,* pronounced "kahm-kah-yee ekh-TAH," in Pushtu.

| | |
|---|---|
| First day of Ramazan | varies |
| Eid al-Fitr (end of Ramazan) | varies |
| Nowruz (New Year's Day) | March 21 |
| Revolution Day | April 27 |
| Workers' Day (Labor Day) | May 1 |
| Eid al-Adha (Feast of the Sacrifice) | varies |
| Ashura (martyrdom of Hussein) | varies |
| Mawleed al-Nabi (birth of the Prophet Muhammad) | varies |
| Jeshn (Independence Day) | August 19 |

powerful religion, long before Islam arrived in Afghanistan. Nowruz was once celebrated on June 21, or the solar equinox, but the date was later changed by the Achaemenids—the first royal dynasty of Persia—to the present date.

Several ancient superstitions are associated with the first day of the New Year. For example, many Afghans believe that on Nowruz, an ugly old woman called Ajuzak roams the world. If rain falls on that day, it is a sign that Ajuzak is washing her hair and the coming year's harvest will be bountiful. Infants are hidden to protect them from Ajuzak's evil eye.

During the celebrations, lavish meals are prepared in Afghan homes. Two dishes, *samanak* and *hafta mewa*, are especially cooked for the occasion. *Samanak*, a dessert made of wheat and sugar, can take more than two days to prepare. *Hafta mewa* consists of seven fruits and nuts to symbolize spring: walnuts, almonds, pistachios, red and green raisins, dried apricots, and a local fruit known as *sanjit* (the dried fruit of the oleaster tree).

On Nowruz, the ceremonial raising of the flag at the tomb of Ali, the Prophet Muhammad's son-in-law, is held at Mazar-i-Sharif. The standard of Ali is raised in the courtyard, and the devout touch the staff—a tradition known as *jandah bala kardan*—hoping to gain merit. The flagstaff remains standing for 40 days, during which thousands of pilgrims flock to Mazar-i-Sharif, including the sick and crippled, hoping to be cured. Forty days after Nowruz, on the day the flag is lowered in Mazar-i-Sharif, a distinctive red species of tulip blooms and then disappears soon after.

During Nowruz, friends and relatives visit one another, wishing everyone longevity, happiness, and productivity. Buzkashi matches are held in Mazar-i-Sharif and other towns. The spring festival of Nowruz is also celebrated on a grand scale in Iran.

## JESHN

One of the few holidays without religious significance in Afghanistan is Jeshn, or Independence Day. This is usually a weeklong celebration in August to mark Afghanistan's independence from the British in May 1919, after the Third Anglo-Afghan War.

The Treaty of Rawalpindi, which granted Afghanistan the freedom to conduct its own foreign affairs, was signed in August 1919. Moreover the harvest ends only in August, giving the rural population more freedom from work to participate in the festivities. Therefore celebrations are usually held at the end of August instead of May.

## OTHER HOLIDAYS

Besides Independence Day and Revolution Day, Afghanistan observes Workers' Day, or Labor Day, which is also a national holiday in many other countries, on the first of May. This is an annual event.

## INTERNET LINKS

**www.afghan-web.com/culture/holidays.html**

This website provides information on the holidays and festivals of Afghanistan.

**www.globalpost.com/photo-galleries/planet-pic/5680454/hajj-2011-muslims-pilgrimage-mecca-photos**

This Global Post site contains photographs depicting Muslims' pilgrimage to Mecca, in the hajj of 2011.

**http://afghanistan.saarctourism.org/festivals.html**

This tourism site provides information and links to holidays and festivals celebrated in Afghanistan, including links to popular sporting events, such as buzkashi, which are often played during festivals.

The national holiday of Revolution Day marks the date April 27, 1978, on which President Daoud was overthrown. Besides the mandatory military parades and displays, Buzkashi matches are held and attended by huge crowds of spectators. All this happens during periods of peace, which have been rare for the war-torn country.

# FOOD

A grocery store in Herat carries all the necessary day-to-day items for the locals.

## 13

A FGHAN CUISINE IS A BLEND of the cooking styles of the many groups that invaded and occupied Afghanistan throughout the centuries. The strongest influences come from its neighbors Iran and India.

Both Iranian food, often regarded as the most refined of all Middle Eastern cuisines, and Indian food, probably the most sophisticated in South Asia, have had the advantage of thousands of years to develop and mature in terms of style and methods of preparations. Afghans have incorporated the best elements of the dishes of these ancient civilizations into their own delightful cuisine that is neither too spicy nor too bland. Its staples are rice and naan bread.

## NAAN

Naan is a flat bread that resembles oversized pancakes. It is usually made from wheat but every kind of grain that can be ground into flour may be used, even peas and mulberries. It is usually baked plain. Sometimes a filling, such as leeks or potatoes, is added for variety.

Naan is usually baked in a tandoor (tehn-DOOR), or clay oven, which is buried in the ground with hot coals under it; it can also be cooked on a hot, circular iron griddle. The nomads often bake it on heated stones. Naan can be prepared in different shapes, too. Oblong is common, although in the north, oval naan is the norm.

This staple is especially important in the villages, where Afghans generally consume more bread than their counterparts in the towns. Town dwellers, who have access to a wider variety of food, consume larger amounts of rice and meat.

• • • • • • • • • • •

Afghan cuisine is largely based upon the nation's chief crops and utilizes wheat, corn, barley, and rice. These staples are accompanied by dairy products and various nuts, vegetables, and fresh and dried fruit. Meat is considered a luxury in many households. Afghans are very hospitable and guests are always welcomed into an Afghan home, even if they arrive without prior notice. The decades of war and conflict combined with severe drought have resulted in poor crops. Afghanistan faces an acute problem of malnutrition and food shortages.

## PILAU

Several varieties of rice are grown in the wetter areas of Afghanistan, including Kunduz, Jalalabad, and Laghman, and meals with rice are as common as those with naan. Rice may be served plain with side dishes, but on special occasions, pilau is also called pilaf, or *pilaw* in Turkish, is served. Pilau is rice cooked with meats or vegetables. A guest at an Afghan's home is invariably invited to share a meal of pilau. Rural Afghans cook the rice with clarified butter (called *ghee* in Hindi), or lard from the tail of a fat-tailed sheep. Urban Afghans, however, are more likely to use vegetable shortening. *Qabili pilau*, Kabul style lamb, and rice pilau is considered best if made with long-grain Basmati rice.

A father serving a meal to his four sons. Typical Afghan meals include staples, such as rice and bread.

Pilau is usually served with a side dish of vegetables and yogurt. Popular vegetables include squash, carrots, eggplant, spinach, potatoes, and peas. Sometimes pickled vegetables, called *toorshi*, are also served. In the cities of Kabul and Jalalabad a special hot chili sauce, called *chutney-morch* (CHOOT-nee-moorch), is a favorite.

## KEBAB

Kebabs are another favorite food of the Afghans. These are usually small cubes of meat skewered with onions, tomatoes, and pieces of fat, then grilled over open charcoal grills.

As with *pilau*, there are many different varieties of kebab. One of the most popular types is *kofta* (kohf-TAH) kebab, which is made with minced meat ground with onions. Another much-loved version is *shami* (SHAW-mee) kebab—minced meat mixed with beaten eggs and mashed potatoes before cooking.

## OTHER FOODS

The Uzbek, Tajik, and other Afghans in the north enjoy pasta dishes, such as *ash* (awsh), a minestrone-type noodle soup. They also have several types of

Afghans usually have only two main meals a day—breakfast and dinner. Leftovers from dinner are often served for breakfast the following day.

## PILAU GALORE!

*The number of ways* pilau *may be cooked is limited only by the chef's imagination. The more popular varieties in Afghanistan are:*

- challaw *(cheh-LAO): Plain rice with a large hunk of mutton or chicken buried within the mound of rice*
- qabili: Pilau *with raisins, shredded carrot, almonds, and pistachios. A guest served* qabili pilau *is held in great respect*
- sabzi: Pilau *with spinach*
- mushung: Pilau *with small green peas*
- yakhni: Pilau *with mutton in steamed rice*
- reshta: Pilau *with eggs*
- baanjaani siyaa: Pilau *with eggplant*
- murgh: Pilau *with chicken*
- naranj *(NAW-rehnj): Sweetish* pilau *with dried orange peel*
- kalapachah: Pilau *with the head (including the animal's eyeballs) and feet of a sheep*
- lawndee *(LOON-dee):* Pilau *with dried meat prepared like jerky; a favorite winter dish*

ravioli, called *ashak* (aw-SHAK), with a variety of fillings, from cheese to meat and leeks. A steamed meat dumpling, called *matoo*, similar to that found in Tibet, is eaten in the north, especially in the winter.

Dairy products are a staple of the Afghans' diet, especially in the diet of nomads and those in rural areas. Milk, not only from cows but also from goats and sheep, is drunk. Besides milk and yogurt, many different types of cheese, both pasteurized and unpasteurized, are made and consumed.

Poultry, including chickens, ducks, turkeys, and guinea fowls, and eggs, are also popular. Freshwater fish from Afghanistan's many rivers has become increasingly popular in recent years. In addition game animals and small wild birds, a prized treat, are hunted and cooked.

Many of Afghanistan's sweets and desserts such as baklava and halvah are similar to those found in India and Pakistan. Besides these, both fresh and dry fruits are abundant. Fruits are of the Mediterranean and temperate

*Shorwa* (shoor-WAH), a gravy usually made with mutton stock, is a favorite dish. Afghans dip their naan in it or drink it as a soup. In the north the Uzbek make their gravy with cattle blood and tomatoes.

*Hospitality is a very important aspect of Afghan culture. In an Afghan home a visitor will be offered the best that the family has, regardless of who the guest is. When one is invited to an Afghan home for tea, it is appropriate to bring a small gift. When invited for meals, one should bring sweets, fruits, or pastries. Gifts should preferably be nicely wrapped. The giver should be subtle and discreet when presenting a gift. Green wrapping paper is preferred for weddings.*

*A male visitor must offer his hand to the host. After shaking hands, the other hand should be placed on the heart and he should give a slight nod or bow. Physical contact between members of the opposite sex is forbidden, so it is not advisable to shake hands with the opposite gender.*

*Shoes should be removed before entering a house. Guests sit cross-legged on cushions and their feet should never point toward another person. The meal is served on plastic tablecloths spread on the floor. Food may be eaten from a common dish. The right hand is used for eating and serving. The left hand should never be used to eat, pass, or receive the food. A guest's plate is refilled as soon as it is empty. Out of politeness, some food should be left on the plate by the guest.*

*Guests are served snacks as well as tea, and their glasses of tea are constantly refilled. If a guest has had enough tea, he can cover his glass with his hand and say* bas, *meaning "enough."*

variety and include melons, apples, pears, apricots, cherries, mulberries, and plums. Nuts, such as pistachios, almonds, and walnuts, are a major part of the Afghan diet and are often carried for quick snacks.

Rice is also cooked and served in several ways in addition to the *pilau* varieties. In convalescence (when recovering from general sickness) it is eaten with lentils as *kichri* (KEEK-ree) or *shuleh* (SHOO-lah), which is a gruel made of rice and split green peas. This is usually served with a mixture of minced meat and ghee or sour cream.

A favorite Afghan rice dish is *dampok* (DAHM-pok), which is simply rice boiled with oil and water.

A pudding called *faluda* (faw-loo-DAH) is prepared by steaming a mixture of wheat flour and milk in a porous bag for 10 to 12 hours. This is then pressed through a machine that makes spaghetti-like strings and served with syrup.

## TEA

Tea is the national drink in Afghanistan and is extremely popular in a land where the consumption of alcohol is prohibited by Islam. It is served with meals and also is drunk in between meals.

Two types of tea are common in Afghanistan—black tea south of the Hindu Kush and green tea in the north. Both kinds of tea are served in teahouses found in towns and villages throughout the country, where Afghan men gather to drink tea and while away their leisure time.

Sugar is considered a luxury, and Afghans have to pay extra to sweeten their tea. Many Afghans soak a sugar cube in the tea, then either eat it or hold it to their mouth as they drink the tea. Unlike many other peoples in South Asia, most Afghans prefer their tea without any milk.

A local Afghan man serves tea at his house in Kabul.

## INTERNET LINKS

**www.muslimrishtey.com/afghanistan_food_recipes/afghan_faluda.php**

This website provides many traditional Afghan recipes, including the recipe for *faluda*.

**www.afghan-web.com/culture/cooking/**

This website introduces you to the unique variety of traditional Afghan cuisine, dishes and different types of food.

**www.afghancooking.net/afghan-culture-unveiled/**

This comprehensive website contains links to Afghan recipes, culture, food markets, holidays, and people. It includes many photographs and interesting facts.

In Afghanistan, as in other Muslim countries, animals must be slaughtered according to prescribed Islamic rituals before their meat may be eaten.

# ASABIA EL AROOS (BRIDE'S FINGERS)

3 cups (750 ml) sugar

1½ cups (375 ml) water

Juice of 1 lemon

½ package (16 ounces, 455 grams) defrosted filo pastry

½ cup (125 ml) almond or pistachio, pulverized in food processor with ⅓ cup (85 ml) sugar

¼ cup (60 ml) unsalted butter, melted

1 egg, lightly beaten

To make the syrup, boil about 2¾ cups (685 ml) of the sugar with the lemon juice and water for about 10 minutes or until the mixture is sticky and golden brown. Preheat the oven to 375°F (190.6°C). Prepare one or two nonstick baking sheets. After cutting the filo pastry dough in half crosswise, and cutting these pieces again into halves, stack and cover the cut rectangular pieces of the pastry with a slightly damp towel to prevent the dough from drying.

Place two rectangular pieces of the cut dough on a clean and dry work surface. With the shorter side of the cut dough facing you, brush the dough lightly with melted butter and place a rounded tablespoonful of the pulverized nut mixture filling across it. Starting from the shorter side, roll up the pastry dough to form a fat cigar-shaped cylinder. Do the same with the rest of the dough. Place the rolled pastry on the baking sheet with the cut edge facing down. Brush the top of the dough with the beaten egg and sprinkle some sugar over the rolls. Bake for 15 to 20 minutes until the dough turns golden brown, and then dip each cooked pastry into the hot sugar syrup. Serve them at room temperature.

# MURGH KEBAB (AFGHAN CHICKEN)

*(Makes 15 sticks)*

2 large garlic cloves

½ (2.5 ml) teaspoon salt

2 cups (500 ml) plain whole milk yogurt

3–4 tablespoons (45–60 ml) pulp and juice of lemon

½ teaspoon (2.5 ml) cracked black pepper

2 pounds (900 g) chicken breast, boneless

Place the salt in a wide shallow bowl and mash this together with the garlic to form a paste. When this is done, add the yogurt, lemon, and pepper to the garlic paste. After removing the skin and extra fat from the chicken meat, flatten it slightly. Next coat the chicken in the yogurt mixture. Place the coated meat in a bowl and cover it. Leave the bowl in the refrigerator overnight.

Skewer the seasoned meat on sticks. Broil or grill the meat 6 inches from the heat for six to eight minutes on each side, or until done. Do not let the chicken breast char. Serve the chicken while it is hot.

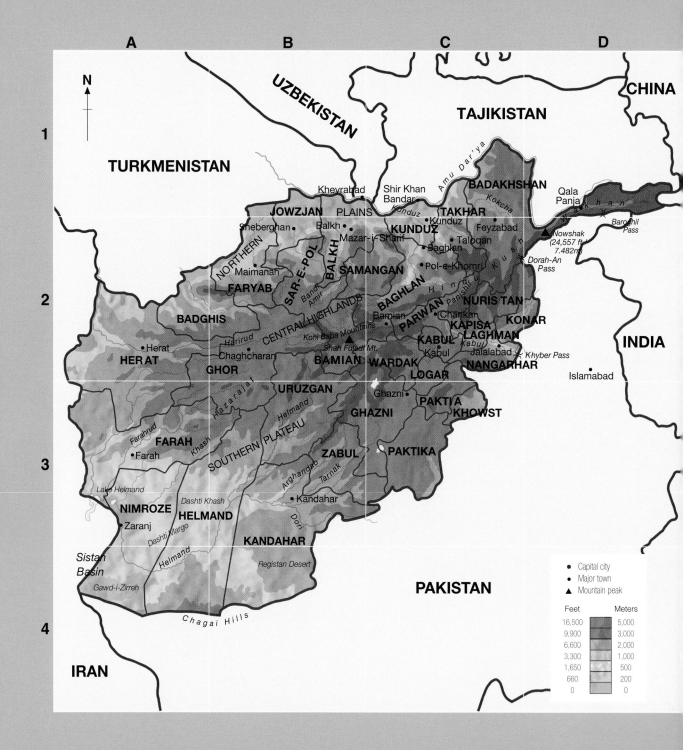

Amu Dar'ya, B1, C1, D1
Arghandab River, B3

Badakhshan, C1—C2, D1—D2
Badghis, A2, B2
Baghlan, B2, C2
Balkh, B1—B2, C1—C2
Bamian, B2, C2
Bandi Amir, B2
Baroghil Pass, D1

Central Highlands, A2—A3, B2—B3, C2
Chagal Hills, A4, B4
Chaghcharan, B2
Charikar, C2
China, D1

Dashti Khash, A3, B3
Dashti Margo, A3—A4
Dorah-An Pass, C2
Dori River, B3, C3

Farah, A3, B3
Farahrud, A3, B2—B3
Faryab, B1—B2
Feyzabad, C2

Gawd-i-Zirreh, A4
Ghazni, B2—B3, C2—C3
Ghor, A2—A3, B2—B3

Harirud River, A2, B2
Hazarajat, A3, B3
Helmand, A3—A4, B3—B4
Helmand River, A3—A4, B1—B4
Herat, A2—A3, B2
Hindu Kush mountain range, B2, C2, D2

India, C4, D1—D4
Iran, A1—A4
Islamabad, D2

Jalalabad, C2
Jowzjan, B1—B2

Kabul, C2
Kabul River, C2
Kandahar, B3—B4, C3
Kapisa, C2
Khash River, A3, B3
Kheyrabad, B1
Khowst, C3
Khyber Pass, C2
Kohi Baba Mountains, B2, C2
Kokcha River, C1—C2
Konar, C2, D2
Kunduz, C1—C2
Kunduz River, C1—C2

Laghman, C2
Lake Helmand, A3
Logar, C2—C3

Maimanah, B2
Mazar-i-Sharif, B2

Nangarhar, C2
Nimroze, A3—A4
Northern Plains, A2, B1—B2, C1—C2
Nowshak, D2
Nuristan, C2, D2

Pakistan, A4, B3—B4, C2—C4, D1—D4
Paktia, C2—C3
Paktika, C3
Panjshir, C2
Parwan, C2
Pol-e-Khomri, C2

Qala Panja, D1

Registan Desert, B3—B4

Samangan, B2, C2
Sar-e-pol, B2

Shah Fuladi Mountain, B2
Sheberghan, B2
Shir Khan Bandar, C1
Sistan Basin, A3—A4
Southern Plateau, A3—A4, B3—B4

Tajikistan, B1, C1, D1, D2
Takhar, C1—C2
Taloqan, C2
Tarnak River, B3, C3
Turkmenistan, A1—A2, B1—B2

Uruzgan, B2—B3
Uzbekistan, A1, B1, C1, D1

Wakhan Corridor, D1—D2
Wardak, B2, C2, C3

Zabul, B3, C3
Zaranj, A3

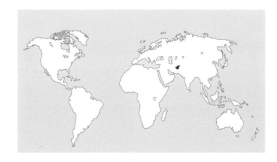

# ECONOMIC AFGHANISTAN

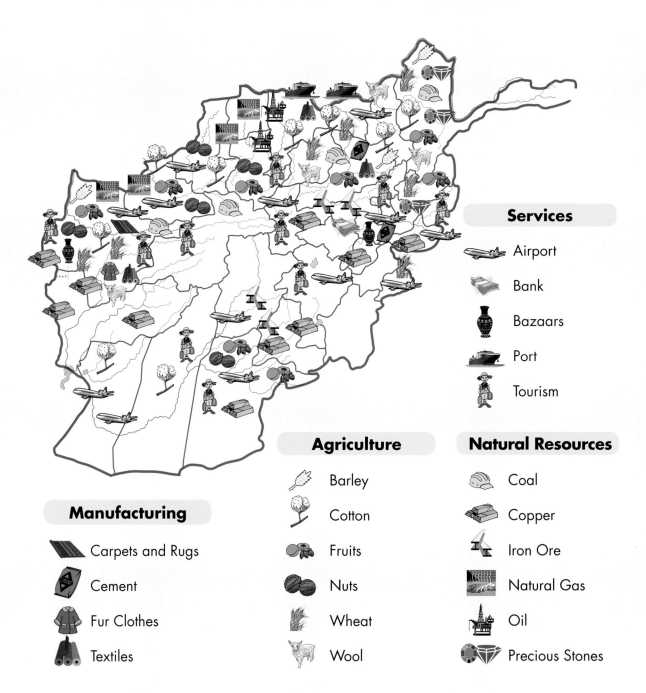

**Services**

- ✈ Airport
- 💵 Bank
- ⚱ Bazaars
- 🚢 Port
- 🧳 Tourism

**Manufacturing**

- Carpets and Rugs
- Cement
- Fur Clothes
- Textiles

**Agriculture**

- Barley
- Cotton
- Fruits
- Nuts
- Wheat
- Wool

**Natural Resources**

- Coal
- Copper
- Iron Ore
- Natural Gas
- Oil
- Precious Stones

# ABOUT THE ECONOMY

## OVERVIEW

After the fall of the Taliban regime, Afghanistan received international aid assistance of $26.7 billion up to 2009. This aid is still ongoing and, combined with the recovery of the agricultural sector and the reestablishment of market institutions in the country, the Afghan economy has improved significantly. Afghanistan is, however, still among the poorest countries of the world. Much of the population lacks the basic necessities of life. Most of its infrastructure needs to be reconstructed, and continued international aid, political stability, and peace are also vital for maintaining progress in Afghanistan. The cultivation of poppies and the opium trade, which account for as much as one-third of GDP, pose serious problems to the country.

## GROSS DOMESTIC PRODUCT (GDP)

$33.5 billion (2012 estimate)

## GDP PER CAPITA

$1,000 (2012 estimate)

## GROWTH RATE

7.1 percent (2011 estimate)

## INFLATION RATE

13.8 percent (2012 estimate)

## CURRENCY

USD1 = 49.88 Afghanis (2012 estimate)
1 Afghani = 100 puls

## WORKFORCE

15 million (2004 estimate)

## UNEMPLOYMENT RATE

15 percent unemployed (2011 estimate) and 35 percent underemployed (2011 estimate)

## POPULATION BELOW POVERTY LINE

36 percent (2008 estimate)

## INDUSTRIES

Small-scale production of textiles, soap, furniture, shoes, fertilizer, apparel, food products, non-alcoholic beverages, mineral water, cement; handwoven carpets; natural gas, coal, copper

## AGRICULTURAL PRODUCTS

Opium, wheat, fruits, nuts, wool, mutton, sheepskins, and lambskins

## NATURAL RESOURCES

Natural gas, petroleum, coal, copper, chromite, talc, zinc, iron ore, salt, sulphur, semiprecious and precious stones

## MAJOR EXPORTS

Karakul sheepskins and wool, hides and pelts, cotton, dried fruit and nuts, fresh fruit, precious and semiprecious gems

## MAJOR IMPORTS

Food, machinery, capital equipment, textiles, and petroleum products

## MAJOR TRADING PARTNERS

Germany, India, Pakistan, Russia, Tajikistan, United States

# CULTURAL AFGHANISTAN

**Masjidi Jam**
Located in Herat, this mosque is an example of the artistic sophistication of Ghorid art. The elaborate 12th-century Jam Tower is located in its garden, and it is one of the world's finest Islamic buildings.

**Bandi Amir**
This is the location of five beautiful clear blue lakes to the west of Bamian, formed by the flow of water over a succession of natural dams. It is the most outstanding site of the natural wonders of Afghanistan.

**Mazar-i-Sharif**
The Blue Mosque houses the shrine of Hazrat Ali, the son-in-law and cousin of the Prophet Muhammad. Thousands of visitors come here to celebrate Now Roz or the Afghan New Year.

**Bamian**
This village is the site of the two famed statues of Buddha, 155 feet and 174 feet (35 m and 53 m) tall, that were hewn into solid rock. They were destroyed by the Taliban but work is under way to reconstruct them.

**Gardens of Babur**
These pleasant gardens were built by Emperor Babur in the 16th century. He died in Agra but asked to be buried here.

**The Citadel**
It has been said that this ancient fort was built by Alexander the Great. It is a reminder of the glorious period of kings, conquerors, and great pageantry, much like the fortress Bala Hissar of Kabul.

**Bazaars**
The colorful and bustling bazaars in Kabul are places where Afghans shop and trade their wares. The ceaseless, uninhibited activity and bargaining, as well as the increasingly wide variety of goods traded, indicate the country's transition to democracy.

**Bala Hisar (Kabul)**
This fortress was the town's main defensive complex. It served as a residence for several rulers, including Babur and Tamerlane. It has figured in much of the country's history.

**Kabul Museum**
Kabul Museum, also known as the National Museum of Afghanistan, had the finest collection of antiquities in Asia. Much of it, unfortunately, has been looted or destroyed by the Taliban.

**Museum of Islamic Art**
This museum has a great collection of objects from the Ghaznavid period, such as mosaic tiles, glass, and bronze.

**Shahri Zohak (The Red City)**
Home to ruins of a cave city ravaged by Genghis Khan, this site is situated on a 350-foot (107-m) high cliff of red stone overlooking the Tagao Valley in Bamian. Due to the red color of the cliffs the city is situated on, it is also known as "The Red City."

**The Mousallah Complex**
The 15th-century complex houses the remains of an old madrasah, or religious school, that is said to be the most beautiful model of the brilliant use of color in architecture. Destruction waged by British troops in the late 19th century and devastation caused by subsequent earthquakes have laid to ruins the 12 minarets that once stood tall in the complex.

**Lashkargah**
The capital of Helmand Province is the site of an ancient city built by Sultan Mahmood Ghaznawi. The ruins of the Masood Palace give an idea of the splendor of what was once the greatest empire of the east.

**Shahri Gholgola (City of Noise)**
This prosperous city from the 5th to the 7th centuries was laid to ruin by Genghis Khan. The "noise" refers to the screams that arose from the massacre.

**The Minarets**
These are the only two remaining minarets that were built in the 12th century. They inspired the Jam Tower, which in turn inspired the Qutub Minar of Delhi, India.

# ABOUT THE CULTURE

**OFFICIAL NAME**
Islamic Republic of Afghanistan

**CAPITAL**
Kabul

**NATIONAL FLAG**
The flag consists of three bands—black, red, and green—and an emblem inscribed with the words "Afghanistan" and "God is great" and "There is no God but Allah, and Muhammad is His messenger."

**POPULATION**
31,108,077 million (2013 estimate)

**AREA**
251,827 square miles (652,230 square km)

**MAJOR RIVERS**
Helmand, Amu Dar'ya, Harirud, Kabul

**PROVINCES**
Badakhshan, Badghis, Baghlan, Balkh, Bamian, Farah, Faryab, Ghazni, Ghor, Helmand, Herat, Jowzjan, Kabul, Kandahar, Kapisa, Khowst, Konar, Kunduz, Laghman, Logar, Nangarhar, Nimroze, Nuristan, Paktia, Paktika, Parwan, Samangan, Sar-e-Pol, Takhar, Uruzgan, Wardak, Zabul

**MAJOR CITIES**
Kandahar, Mazar-i-Sharif, Herat, Ghazni, Jalalabad, Farah, Shibarghan, Charikar, Kunduz, Maimanah, Puli Khumri

**ETHNIC GROUPS**
Pashtun 42 percent; Tajik 27 percent; Hazara 9 percent; Uzbek 9 percent; Aimak 4 percent; Turkmen 3 percent; Baloch 2 percent; and others 4 percent

**OFFICIAL LANGUAGES**
Pashtu and Dari (Afghan Persian)

**MAJOR RELIGIONS**
Islam: Sunni Muslims, Shi'a Muslims

**LIFE EXPECTANCY**
49 years male; 52 years female (2013 estimate)

**FERTILITY RATE**
5.64 children per woman (2012 estimate)

**BIRTH RATE**
39.30 births per 1,000 Afghans (2013 estimate)

**INFANT MORTALITY RATE**
121.63 deaths per 1,000 live births (2013 estimate)

**DEATH RATE**
14.59 deaths per 1,000 Afghans (2013 estimate)

**LITERACY RATE**
Population: 28.1 percent; male 43 percent; female 12.6 percent (2010 estimates)

# TIMELINE

| IN AFGHANISTAN | IN THE WORLD |
|---|---|

**328 B.C.**
Alexander the Great captures Bactria (Balkh).

**A.D. 642**
The Arabs introduce Islam to Afghanistan.

**998–1030**
Mahmud of Ghazni turns Ghazni into a great cultural center, and base for forays into India.

**1206–1368**
Genghis Khan unifies the Mongols and starts conquest of the world. At its height, the Mongol Empire under Kublai Khan stretches from China to Persia and parts of Europe and Russia.

**1370**
Afghanistan is incorporated into the empire of Tamerlane, whose Timurid dynasty ends after 100 years. Their capital is at Herat.

**1500s**
Babur, the founder of India's Moghul dynasty, moves the capital to Kabul.

**1747**
Ahmad Shah Durrani (born Ahmad Khan Abdali) creates a single Afghanistan.

**1776**
U.S. Declaration of Independence

**1838–42**
The First Anglo-Afghan War is waged.

**1878–80**
The Second Anglo-Afghan War breaks out.

**1914**
World War I begins.

**1919**
Amanullah comes into power and launches the Third Anglo-Afghan War to gain independence.

**1919–29**
King Amanullah introduces reforms for modernization and secularism but abdicates in 1929. Kabul falls to forces of Habibullah, also called Bacheh Saqow, a Tajik brigade. Mohammad Nadir Khan, also known as Nadir Shah, a cousin of Amanullah, later defeats Bacheh Saqow in October and is declared king.

**1933**
Mohammad Nadir Khan is assassinated.

**1933–73**
Zahir Shah rules.

**1939–45**
World War II

**1973**
Mohammed Daud Khan seizes power in a military coup and declares a republic.

**1978**
A bloody coup by the People's Democratic Party breaks out. Daud is killed. Nur Mohammed Taraki becomes prime minister.

**1979**
After a shootout in the palace, Hafizullah Amin takes over from Taraki, who is killed. The Soviet Union invades Afghanistan. Hafizullah is killed, and Babrak Karmal is installed as president. The Muslim groups unite to form the mujahideen (guerrilla warriors) and launch resistance to the Soviet invasion.

| IN AFGHANISTAN | IN THE WORLD |
|---|---|
| **1986** Karmal is replaced by Najibullah. | |
| **1988** A ceasefire is declared. The Geneva Accord is signed, and the governments of Pakistan and Afghanistan are guaranteed noninterference from the United States and the Soviet Union. | |
| **1992** The communist regime of Najibullah is overthrown by the mujahideen. Civil war erupts. | **1997** Hong Kong is returned to China. |
| **1994–98** The Taliban captures Kandahar and Kabul. | |
| **2001** The United States launches a military campaign after the September 11 terrorist attacks, and the Taliban government is ousted from Kabul. The Bonn Agreement is signed. | **2001** Terrorists crash planes into New York, Washington D.C., and Pennsylvania. **2003** War in Iraq begins. |
| **2004** A democratic presidential election is conducted. Hamid Karzai is elected president. | **2004** Eleven Asia countries are hit by giant tsunami, killing at least 225,000 people. |
| **2005** General elections are held and the National Assembly is inaugurated. | **2005** Hurricane Katrina devastates the Gulf Coast of the United States. |
| **2006** NATO assumes responsibility for security across the whole country. | |
| **2009** NATO countries pledge to increase military and other commitments; President Barack Obama says United States will begin to withdraw U.S. troops by 2011. | **2009** Outbreak of flu virus H1N1 around the world. |
| **2010** Operation Moshtarak launched by NATO-led forces in a bid to secure government control of Helmand Province; NATO agrees plan to hand control of security to Afghan forces by 2014. | |
| **2011** Afghanistan and India sign a strategic partnership to increase cooperation as relations with Pakistan worsen; President Karzai wins the endorsement of tribal elders to negotiate a 10-year military partnership with the United States—the proposed pact will enable U.S. troops to remain after 2014 when foreign troops are due to leave the country; Pakistan and the Taliban boycott the Bonn Conference on Afghanistan in December. | **2011** Twin earthquake and tsunami disasters strike northeast Japan, leaving more than 14,000 dead and thousands more missing. |
| **2012** Taliban agree to open an office in Dubai as a move toward peace talks with the United States and Afghan government. | |

# GLOSSARY

*Azan* (ah-ZAHN)
The call to prayer.

*baadi sadu beest roz*
Strong winds along the Iran-Afghanistan border that are also known as the wind of 120 days.

Buzkashi
Game in which teams of horsemen compete to carry a headless goat or calf over a goal line.

*chadari* (chawdari)
Traditional garment worn in public that covers a woman from head to foot.

*jangal* (jehng-EHL)
Forest or wooded area.

jihad
Muslim holy war against people who are a threat to the Islamic religion.

*jooyi* (joo-YEE)
Artificially made pools or streams.

Loya Jirga
A grand assembly where tribal elders discuss and settle national issues.

Meli Shura
Highest legislative body of Afghanistan.

mujahideen
"Holy warriors" of Islam or Muslim guerrilla fighters.

mullah
Muslim teacher or scholar.

*pahlwani* (pahl-wah-NEE)
Wrestling.

pilau
Rice cooked with meats or vegetables.

posteen
A coat made of sheepskin or leather.

purdah
Seclusion of Muslim women.

*Pashtunwali* (PUHSH-toon-WAH-lee)
Honor code of conduct or Pashtun tribal law code upheld by most Afghans.

*Salat* (saw-LAWT)
Prayers.

*Shahadat* (sheh-hah-DEHT)
The belief in Allah as the only God, and in the Prophet Mohammed as His messenger.

*tandoor* (tehn-DOOR)
A traditional clay oven used to bake naan.

Wolesi Jirga
House of the People, or House of Representatives.

yurt
A portable, domed tent of skins or felt used by semi-nomads.

*zakat* (zeh-KAHT)
Alms given to the poor every year.

# FOR FURTHER INFORMATION

## BOOKS

Barfield, Thomas. *Afghanistan: A Cultural and Political History*. New Jersey: Princeton University Press, 2010.

Bryson, Bill. *In a Sunburned Country*. New York, NY: Broadway Books, 2001.

Ellis, Deborah. *The Breadwinner Trilogy*. Toronto: Groundwood Books, 2009.

Ewans, Martin. *Afghanistan: A Short History of Its People and Politics*. New York, NY: Harper Perennial, 2002.

Loyn, David. *In Afghanistan: two hundred years of British, Russian and American occupation*. New York: Palgrave Macmillan, 2009.

Rashid, Ahmed. *Taliban: Militant Islam, Oil and Fundamentalism in Central Asia*. New Haven, CT: Yale University Press, 2010.

Staples, Suzanne Fisher. *Under the Persimmon Tree*. New York: Farrar Straus and Giroux (Books for Young Readers), 2008.

Stewart, Rory. *The Places in Between*. Boston, MA: Mariner Books, 2006.

## DVDS

*Afghanistan Revealed: The Untold Story of a Land*. National Geographic, 2010.

*Restrepo: One Platoon, One Valley, One Year*. Virgil Films and Entertainment. Directed by Sebastian Junger and Tim Hetherington, 2010.

*Rethink Afghanistan*. Directed by Robert Greenwald, 2009.

*Ross Kemp: The Afghanistan Collection*. BBC, 2012.

## MUSIC

*Teahouse Music of Afghanistan*. Smithsonian Folkways, 2010.

*Tracks in the Dust-Songs from Afghanistan*. CDBY, 2011.

# BIBLIOGRAPHY

## BOOKS

Barfield, Thomas. *Afghanistan: A Cultural and Political History*. Princeton, NJ: Princeton University Press, 2012.

Kazem, Halima. *Countries of the World: Afghanistan*. Tarrytown, NY: Marshall Cavendish Corporation, 2010.

McCord, Kate. *In the Land of Blue Burqas*. Chicago: Moody Publishers, 2012.

Tanner, Stephen. *Afghanistan: A Military History from Alexander the Great to the War Against the Taliban*. Cambridge, MA: Da Capo Press, 2009.

## WEBSITES

Afghanistan Business Culture and Etiquette. www.kwintessential.co.uk

Afghanistan Online. www.afghan-web.com

Afghanistan's Environmental Casualties. www.motherjones.com

Asia Society Curriculum. http://asiasociety.org/

BBC: History of Afghanistan. www.bbc.co.uk

CIA: The World Fact Book—Afghanistan. www.cia.gov/cia/publications/factbook

CIC Wildlife. www.cic-wildlife.org

Kabul Museum. http://portal.unesco.org

NationMaster.com—Encyclopedia. www.nationmaster.com

# INDEX

# INDEX